The Abundant Garden

The Abundant Garden

A practical guide to growing a regenerative home garden

Niva & Yotam Kay

—

Of Pakaraka Permaculture

ALLEN & UNWIN
SYDNEY • MELBOURNE • AUCKLAND • LONDON

First published in 2021

Copyright © Niva and Yotam Kay, 2021

Photography copyright © Niva Kay and Jane Ussher

Jane Ussher
Front cover and pages 5, 6, 9, 10, 13, 14, 15, 23, 27, 29, 31, 35, 26, 37, 49, 50, 51, 57, 65, 78, 71, 72, 73, 84, 86, 91, 95, 96, 97, 106, 111, 112, 119, 121, 122, 123, 141, 143, 146, 149, 152, 154, 160, 163, 171, 169, 181, 183, 189, 208, 218, 219, 229, 237, 246, 258, 259, 262, 265, 272, 275, 282, 283, 286, 298, 299, 303, 310, 320

Niva Kay
Back cover and pages 20, 27, 33, 42, 55, 58, 75, 78, 82, 90, 101, 102, 108, 113, 114, 117, 125, 129, 133, 135, 136, 138, 139, 142, 147, 153, 156, 158, 162, 166, 168, 173, 174, 176, 177, 178, 183, 186, 191, 192, 194, 196, 197, 199, 200, 202, 204, 206, 217, 221, 223, 225, 233, 232, 235, 236, 240, 257, 260, 270, 276, 290, 293, 306, 307, 308, 313

Illustration copyright © Bianca Rocca

Allen & Unwin
Level 2, 10 College Hill
Auckland 1011, New Zealand
Phone: (64 9) 377 3800
Email: info@allenandunwin.com
Web: www.allenandunwin.co.nz

83 Alexander Street
Crows Nest NSW 2065, Australia
Phone: (61 2) 8425 0100

A catalogue record for this book is available
from the National Library of New Zealand

ISBN 978 1 98854 771 8

Cover and internal design by Megan van Staden
Set in 12/16 pt Adobe Caslon Pro
Printed and bound in China by C & C Offset Printing Co., Ltd.

10 9 8 7 6 5 4 3

Dedicated to our grandmothers

The Abundant Garden

Contents

Introduction

Whether you're just starting out or are an experienced gardener, this book is packed with insights that will support you in your growing journey.

We are delighted to share with you our love for gardening, and the pleasure of eating home-grown food. We have taken all our knowledge and experience from years of working and learning as organic market gardeners, and are incredibly excited to offer it to you in this comprehensive book about regenerative home gardening.

The Abundant Garden

We love making gardening accessible, fun, and attainable for as many people as possible. Over the years, we have taught the art of organic and regenerative vegetable gardening (both home gardening and organic market gardening) to thousands of people, which has helped us to identify what information gardeners might find useful and relevant. Every chapter in the book is written with you in mind, as we demystify what is involved in creating and maintaining a productive and regenerative vegetable garden.

> We work with nature, enhancing the soil life and fertility, and providing plants with what they need to thrive.

Since we started our gardening journey in 2005, we have studied and practised permaculture, regenerative farming and homesteading. We have experimented with a variety of gardening techniques, eventually leading to the systems we use today. The information we share in this book is based on our experience working with nature, enhancing the soil life and fertility, and providing plants with what they need to thrive. The information is also grounded in the latest scientific research on soil health and ecological and regenerative practices. Vegetable gardening in this way repeatedly demonstrates that every loved garden bed can produce high-yielding, resilient, nourishing and delicious vegetables year after year.

In 2014, our family was privileged to join Jeanette Fitzsimons and Harry Parke at Pakaraka Farm, an organic farm in the Kauaeranga Valley, Thames, Aotearoa New Zealand. Here at this beautiful spot, we established the Pakaraka Permaculture Market Garden and Education Centre for Regenerative Living, with the burning desire to feed our community with the best food we can grow and share this knowledge with other keen gardeners. Our market garden is a diversified organic operation, producing over 8500 kg (18,700 lb) of fresh produce a season from a quarter acre of land.

This book provides simple, reliable strategies and techniques, covering all aspects of home gardening to maximise your ability to feed yourself and share the abundance with those around you. We cover all of our favourite crops, and you will find helpful charts

Left Harry, Niva, Yotam, Lily and Dina in Harry's garden.

with the information you need to plan and plant your garden year-round. We have also included a chapter on microgreens and on our favourite recipes for ferments, preserves and pickles so you can stock the pantry with your garden's bounty.

Our gardening approach seeks to improve the garden and soil ecosystems with every season, contributing to biodiversity, carbon sequestration and mitigating climate change while producing increasing yields and healthier crops. We strongly believe that growing food at home does more than increase your food resilience and provide delicious produce. Regenerative gardening is one of the most meaningful actions communities and individuals can take to combat climate change as well as supporting your mental and physical well-being.

We hope this book will be a useful companion throughout your gardening journey. You can also follow us on Facebook and Instagram at Pakaraka Permaculture, and visit our website at pakarakafarm.co.nz to stay up to date with our news.

Happy gardening,
Niva and Yotam

> Our gardening approach seeks to improve the garden and soil ecosystems with every season . . .

Chapter 1

Designing your vegetable garden

Every garden is unique, because each garden is the coming together of a special landscape of people, land, history, microclimate and resources.

This chapter explores the basic principles of creating a highly productive, regenerative vegetable garden. A regenerative gardening approach is holistic, and considers the long-term consequences of gardening on the soil and the garden's ecosystem, aiming to improve soil biodiversity and the use of resources. In chapter 3, we explain in detail how to go about making your garden a reality.

The process of designing your garden, in a way that reflects your needs and desires, includes examining what makes you tick. Identifying your core values and designing your garden around them will make sure the garden meets your needs. The better job you do at this, the happier you will be with the results.

Keeping a garden diary

Before we start, we'd like to recommend keeping a garden diary to record as much information as you can about your gardening journey. It can be a physical notebook or an electronic folder on your computer with various documents in it.

A garden diary is the place to record any gardening activities you have undertaken during the season. It is especially useful when trying something new, when something unusual happens, when recording your experiments and to keep track of where your main crops have been planted for crop-rotation purposes. It is also a useful place to record weather data, such as the first and last frosts, which can help you plan next season's planting schedule. As the saying goes, writing is the opposite of forgetting.

The best place for a garden

Determining the location of your garden is probably the most significant decision you will need to make. Where you choose to establish your garden is going to determine its success and ease of maintenance. Taking some time at this point for observation will lead to a better garden design. So, make yourself a cup of tea and spend some time observing your garden.

The perfect garden location is hard to find, so most of us will need to make some compromises. Don't be discouraged; on the contrary, you are learning to pay attention to your garden, and this habit will set you up for success throughout your gardening life.

If you have an already established garden, we hope this information will help you notice some positives about your garden's location, and perhaps you will find you can tweak a few things to help your plants thrive even more.

Sun
Direct sunlight is the power supply for your garden. Although leafy greens can grow well in low-light conditions (as little as three to five hours a day), *most vegetables require eight or more hours of direct sunlight to thrive.*

Ideally, your garden will be north-facing (for gardens in the southern hemisphere; south-facing for the northern hemisphere), with only minor shaded areas throughout the year. If you need to make a choice, morning light is more important than afternoon light, because the early-morning sun dries the leaves of the plants, and reduces the chance for fungal diseases to take hold.

If you do have shaded areas, you can use them to your advantage. For example, in the summer, leafy greens do better if they are partially shaded.

In urban areas especially, you can also use walls to your advantage. Walls can reflect light onto your plants, increasing the amount of sunlight they receive.

Shelter

As we want our plants to thrive, we are trying to create conditions that let them concentrate their energy on growing. Wind protection is vital; plants will dedicate a significant amount of energy to developing a strong stem and general sturdiness to survive in the wind, at the expense of their potential yield. Wind also steals the heat and moisture from the soil, cooling and drying it, which make growing conditions even tougher.

To shelter your plants, you can plant a perennial hedge, grow a bed of tall, hardy annuals or install a windbreak fabric. Or do all of these! The idea is not to completely block the airflow, as it is essential for a healthy garden for air to move around and to avoid stagnant air pockets. The best windbreaks allow 30–50 per cent of the air to pass through them. Unlike solid walls, windbreaks are designed to absorb and slow down the wind, but not block it completely. When choosing windbreak plants, look for fast-growing natives that do well in your area.

The guiding principle is that for every metre (3.3 feet) of hedge height, the wind effect is reduced for 10 metres (33 feet) of garden.

PREVAILING WINDS

Above A native windbreak reducing the impact of the prevailing winds on the garden. Note that the garden beds are oriented east to west for maximum sun hours.

Distance from shrubs and trees

Trees and shrubs are significant in creating a healthy ecosystem, but they should be kept away from the veggie garden. Tree roots that reach the garden will spread, taking away water and nutrients from your vegetables, making it harder from them to thrive. Most trees send roots out as far as twice their height. Therefore a 4 metre (13 feet) high tree will send its roots as far as 8 metres (26 feet) away from its trunk. With the temptation of moisture and nutrients in the vegetable garden, some tree roots will reach even further.

Access

'The best fertiliser for a garden is the gardener's feet' is probably our favourite garden saying, because it highlights the close relationship between the gardener and the garden. When you visit your garden often, you notice and observe what's happening to your plants. You learn how they look when they are thriving, and when they seem in need of watering or are under pressure from pests.

To make sure you stay connected to what's happening in your

garden, locate it in the most central place you can. In permaculture design, we call this 'Zone 1', the areas you visit at least once a day. We recommend not to place your vegetable garden at the back of your section, because as the saying goes, 'out of sight, out of mind'. Ideally, place the garden close to your main path so that it is easy and convenient to reach.

Slope

The sweet spot for a vegetable garden is on a moderate 5 per cent slope, to allow for good natural drainage and ease of gardening, and north-facing (south-facing in the northern hemisphere) so it can enjoy the most sunlight hours. At our main gardens we have neither a gentle slope nor a north-facing garden, and it didn't deter us at all.

Our Pakaraka gardens are a mixture of flat land and slope. If you are gardening on a slope greater than 10 per cent, which means a 10 cm height difference over a 1 metre length (4 inches over 3.3 feet), it is beneficial to terrace the slope or to level the platform. Terracing helps to hold the soil and protect it from eroding, and also creates a flat garden bed that helps spread the water more evenly and is more convenient to work with.

Forming the beds along the contour of the land, perpendicular to the slope, is key when working with slopes. When beds are positioned on the contour, the flow of the water is slowed down, which helps to capture more water as well as preventing soil erosion. If garden beds are not planted on the contour of the land, water picks up speed and takes some of the topsoil with it, creating water channels and gullies on its way down the slope.

We like to do most of the work on terraced and contoured beds from the path below them, which makes it easier to reach and puts less stress on the back. Careful bed placement and terracing are some of the best investments you can make in a sloping garden to retain your topsoil and for ease of work.

Topsoil

Each garden has its unique soil profile. When a site is developed, often the topsoil is disturbed. If your garden site is temporary, such as when renting, we recommend that your garden has a minimum

Below Lettuces planted in a no-dig bed.

of 20 cm (8 inches) of topsoil, preferably with no rocks.

If you don't have much topsoil, don't worry. You can either import new topsoil or build it up over time from scratch. It may not be ideal, but you absolutely can create a thriving garden regardless of the soil conditions you start with.

Drainage

The roots of your plants need air. To guarantee that, good drainage is critical because a waterlogged bed will create an anaerobic environment. While you can improve the drainage of the beds through the regenerative cultivation techniques detailed in chapter 3, it is vital that your garden is in a place where water doesn't pool, and there is no or very low risk of flooding.

Water access

Water is the most essential input to a garden, especially during the summer. Make it easy to water your garden by making sure there is a tap nearby. In chapter 8, we cover this topic in-depth, including estimated water needs for gardens and some irrigation options and layouts.

Toxicity

Although most places are safe to garden, some are not. See if you can learn about the history of your land, and if possible, ask around the neighbourhood about concerns regarding historic land pollution from mining, industry or horticulture. Generally, chemical sprays and synthetic fertiliser used on paddocks won't cause an ongoing problem, at least compared to land that has been used for orcharding or cropping, which would have been heavily sprayed.

If you are concerned, you can send a soil sample to a lab that specialises in soil toxicity tests.

Storing tools and supplies

Most gardens don't need much extra room for storage and supplies, but still, it is handy to think about what supplies you will use and where you will keep them. For example, whether you make your own compost or buy it in, it makes sense to place the compost heap as close as possible to the garden to avoid double handling and unnecessary work.

A few quality hand tools are all you need to grow an abundance of produce. High-quality tools are more pleasant to work with, though any tool will do the job. Place your tools in an easily accessible spot, preferably under cover, so that they can last for many years. Keep other supplies such as woodchips, mulch, organic fertilisers and liquid feeds away from the sun and rain. Hoops and cloches will also need a place to hang while not in use.

In our second year of commercial growing at Pakaraka, we grew $50,000 worth of vegetables using a fork, two hoes, a shovel, a rake, a trowel, a few buckets and a wheelbarrow. That's it.

As our gardens are substantial in size, we now use a broad-fork and a wide rake, which covers double the area with the same action, making our bed preparation a little bit easier.

Room for a small tunnel house?

A tunnel house is by no means a necessity, but it can bring another level of joy and productivity to your gardening. A tunnel house allows you to propagate all your own seedling transplants and have a few tomato plants that will keep on producing when the outdoor plants finish their season in the summer, as well as undercover lettuce and other greens in the winter.

Sizing your garden for your lifestyle

If you are just starting out, it is a good idea to start with a small garden, which is much easier to establish and maintain. Taking care of a couple of beds can provide a lot of vegetables . . . and a lot of learning.

As your skills and confidence grow, a more extensive garden will be able to supply you with more fresh produce for an extended time throughout the year. When you are deciding where to locate your garden, keep a possible future expansion in mind.

A home garden can contribute much to your quality of life and the environment. We highly recommend planning for expanding

your garden over time. Starting out with a 10 square metre garden (107 square feet) will provide you with heaps of fresh produce. If you want to grow most of the fresh vegetables and herbs needed for a few people or a family, a 50 to 100 square metre garden (538 to 1076 square feet) is worth aiming for.

The following table illustrates the amount of time it takes to maintain a vegetable garden with a regenerative gardening system (described later in this book).

Weekly time investment depending on a gardener's skill level and garden growing area

	10 square metres (107 square feet)	25 square metres (270 square feet)	50 square metres (538 square feet)	100 square metres (1076 square feet)
Beginner gardener	1.5 hours a week	3 hours a week	5 to 6 hours a week	7 to 9 hours a week
Medium-skilled gardener	1 hour a week	2 hours a week	3 to 4 hours a week	5 to 6 hours a week
Experienced gardener	45 minutes a week	1.5 hours a week	2 to 3 hours a week	4 to 5 hours a week

This table is only a guide, as many variables will affect your time in the garden, such as the season, crop choices and watering system. These time estimates have some seasonal variation, and can either be divided over a few days during the week or a concentrated weekend activity (except for summer watering, which needs to be spread out over the week).

Plan your garden size to the amount of time you have available and want to spend caring for it. Otherwise, the garden work might well overwhelm you. Remember to start small!

Another way to think about sizing your garden is to consider how much produce you would like to harvest.

The following table gives an estimate of the yield different-sized gardens can provide.

Spending time in the garden
Cultivating a healthy and productive garden is not a result of mastering one aspect of growing, it is about doing a lot of small things well. Observing and interacting with your soil and plants is the key to successful vegetable gardening. The best way to be attuned to the many nuances in the garden is by spending regular time in the garden.

Yearly yield per square metre of growing area categorised by the gardener's skill level

	Yearly yield per 10 square metres of growing area (107 square feet)
Beginner gardener	40 to 60 kg (88 to 132 lbs)
Medium-skilled gardener	60 to 80 kg (132 to 176 lbs)
Experienced gardener	80 to 100 kg (176 to 220 lbs)

These estimates are averages, and take into account crop rotation and growing a variety of crops.

This chart also shows that it's well worth investing in your passion for vegetable gardening. Think about how much money you would have spent on this amount of vegetables; we estimate $500 to $1,000 per 10 square metres (107 square feet) a year. Not many hobbies can support your well-being, have a beneficial contribution to combating climate change, and give you tomatoes!

Garden layout

Our garden is also our art. We have designed many gardens in various shapes and sizes over the years. It can be a lot of fun creating curves and unusual shapes for garden beds, rather than sticking to straight rows. But really, the most efficient layout for a garden is standardised straight beds, and that's what we currently prefer. We find ways to express ourselves within these straight bed layouts through our crop choices, placement and by incorporating flowers among the vegetables.

Be flexible in your garden design and make sure it fits your needs. Talk it through with your gardening partners and share this process with them. At the end of this chapter, you will find a set of questions to help you collaborate on a garden design that meets everyone's needs.

Permanent garden beds

Given our soil is the basis for our success, we need to treat it with love and care. Avoid stepping on and compacting your beds as much as possible. Once your beds are established where and how you want them to be, at ground level or raised, don't change them. The garden bed should continue to be the growing area, and the path should remain the path.

By creating permanent beds, you can concentrate your compost applications and get rid of the hardpan, which is common in most soils. Hardpan is a hard layer, often clay, that occurs below the soil and affects its drainage. Without a hardpan, your plants will be able to send their roots deeper, which will, in turn, allow you to increase your planting density and obtain better plant health and yield. We explain how we go about achieving that in chapter 3.

Standard bed width and length

We recommend designing the measurements of your beds with the same width and length.

The width of the beds should be set so that you could easily reach the middle of the bed from the paths without overstretching your back. This is true for both raised beds and when growing at ground level. For shorter people, the bed width could be 80 cm (32 inches), and for taller people, it might be 100 cm (40 inches).

There are a few other consequences from your garden-bed width. The wider the bed, the better the bed's microclimate and water retention. But, if the bed is narrower, it is easier to move around, straddle the beds, plant, prepare and harvest.

Your beds can be any length that works for you and your space. When using cloches, cut the covers to the same length and width so they can be used on any bed in the field.

Paths

The main path leading to the garden should be wide enough to wheel a wheelbarrow load of compost comfortably. Once you are in the garden, unless it is especially big, the other paths can be much narrower.

The main advantage of narrow paths is that by occupying a

Above Scabiosa.

Below
Strawflower.

small space, they can easily be maintained and weeded while taking up less growing space. The other significant advantage is that by keeping the growing beds close to one another, they create a better microclimate for plant growth. We find that with 30–40 cm (12–14 inches) paths, we can easily walk around the garden, bend over, squat and place a bucket or basket on the path. Because our gardens are at ground level, we can also take a wheelbarrow on the path, which we use to spread compost, or gather leftover garden crops on the way to the compost heap.

Edging

We find that creating permanent garden edging that keeps the grass out helps a lot in keeping the garden beds free of weeds. We either use ground-durable timber such as 50 mm x 150 mm (2 inch x 6 inch) boards of macrocarpa or eucalyptus, or lay down woven landscape fabric. We use the woven landscape fabric (also known as weedmat) that is UV stabilised and has a 90 gsm grade or higher. This quality of weedmat can last for 10 to 20 years.

Other options for edging are paving or planting low perennials, such as herbs or even comfrey, and keeping the ground around them well mulched with woodchips.

If your beds are significantly raised, it should be fine to simply keep the paths mulched or mowed short.

Wild areas

Establishing hedgerows, undisturbed patches or wild garden areas can add a lot to your garden's ecosystem health. They provide permanent habitats and shelter to beneficial predatory animals, such as birds, lizards and insects. They can also double as windbreaks, and can be interplanted with productive edible perennials, medicinal herbs or cut flowers.

Pest proofing

The types of pests you will face in your garden depend on whether you live in an urban or rural environment. If you are not familiar with the garden pests around you, use it as an opportunity to reach out to a vegetable gardener in your neighbourhood and ask them to share their expertise.

Right Luna in the wild garden alongside the entrance path.

The Abundant Garden

Designing your vegetable garden

In some cases, such as in inner-city gardens, you will have very little pest pressure. Rurally, you will most likely find at least one of the following munching on your plants: possums, rabbits, quails, rats or sparrows. We will talk about solutions to these pests in chapter 10, but keep in mind you might need to fence your garden from rabbits or use bird netting to keep your precious veggies safe.

Using the edge

Every season we find new ways to use the edge area in and around our gardens. The place where two habitats meet, such as the garden bed and the wall, is an opportunity to create something special. A wall might be used for trellising or to reflect extra light onto the bed, a semi-shaded patch in summer can be used to grow lettuce and the edge of a bed close to an open area can be used to let pumpkins sprawl.

Materials

Think about what materials are readily available for you to use. What repurposed, recycled or sustainably sourced materials can you use to create your garden? What materials are you comfortable to work with? Do you know of someone who can lend you a helping hand? Untreated hardwood is our personal preference for edging, raised beds and terracing. Other great options are rocks and stones, stabilised adobe and recycled plastic edging products.

Incremental design

While it's always a good idea to start small, your design will develop and evolve over time no matter the size of garden you choose. It's easier to make changes when growing in the soil without raised beds. Take the time to reflect on what you've learned from caring for your garden; you can always go back to the drawing board and redesign the garden's paths and beds.

Neighbours

Your garden extends beyond the soil it is grown in. It is affected by your bioregion, and by your neighbours. It could be affected by spray drift from a nearby farmer, pollution from a major highway, problematic pets or shade from trees grown in the neighbouring property.

Right Wheel-hoe resting on untreated wood edging.

There are also positive aspects of having neighbours; sharing your garden abundance with neighbours is one of life's true delights. Ask around to see if there are local crop swaps or community shelves. Good relationships with your neighbours can also mean having a helping hand watering your garden when you are away.

Take time to map out your neighbour's situation in relation to your garden so that you can factor that into your design.

Climate, climate disruption and building resilience

Most vegetables can be grown in most climates. As you will learn in this book, vegetables originated from different parts of the world and therefore thrive under different conditions. By being attuned to the plants' needs, you can increase the plant health and the productivity of your garden. Part of the beauty of home gardening is in growing and eating seasonal vegetables, matching a plant's preferences with your local conditions. Your climate will dictate when you should be busy in the garden, and when to take it easy, when you need to be around to water, and when you should cover your veggies with cloches to protect from heavy rain or frosts.

Unfortunately, with the increasing effects of climate disruption, the weather is becoming less and less predictable. As gardeners, we need to create resilient systems to allow us to have food security. Identify the advantages of your location and climate, as well as its weaknesses in relations to growing food. Depending on your situation this might include installing an extra water tank to capture winter rains or building a tunnel house to keep summer vegetables dry if you live in an area with wet summers.

Exercise: Designing your garden

This set of questions can help you imagine what your dream garden might look like. If you are planning your garden with a partner or with your family, it's a good idea for all of you to discuss what you value in a garden. Start by letting each person write down their answers. You can include sketches or reference photos from other gardens that inspire you.

- **Aesthetics.** What does a visually pleasing veggie garden look like for you?
- **Self-expression.** What would make you see yourself in your garden?
- **Productivity.** How much do you hope to grow? Are you looking for a diversity of crops and varieties or do you want to focus on a few favourites? Do you hope to be self-sufficient with your vegetables? Do you expect to grow many staples (such as potatoes and kumara) or do you mainly want the added flavours of homegrown herbs, fresh greens and salads? Do you want to grow seasonal crops or push the boundaries by investing more effort to extend the season?
- **Commitment.** Would you visit your garden most days of the week or only occasionally?
- **Accessibility.** Do you have any special needs in terms of accessibility that can affect the design of the garden, such as wider paths, raised beds, availability of resting places or ergonomics?
- **Kid-friendly.** Do you want your garden to be kid-friendly?
- **Heritage.** Is there something from your culture or ancestral heritage that you would like to incorporate in the garden? It could be a feature, such as a particular vegetable, flower or herb, or it might be an integral part of your garden layout and overall design.

Once you have identified your main priorities, review your notes, and if relevant, compare them with your gardening partners. What are the most important needs that came out of this exercise? Use them to make decisions regarding the design of your garden, together with the concepts illustrated in this chapter.

Chapter 2
Cultivating healthy soils

Soil is at the heart of an organic garden. Take care of the soil, and the soil will nourish your plants. In this chapter, we explore the characteristics of a 'healthy soil', and learn how to improve it. The result will be healthy plants and delicious, nutritious vegetables.

What is soil?

Soil is made up of a mixture of eroded rocks, decomposed and decayed organic matter from different origins (such as fallen leaves, animal manure and the remains of dead creatures), gases, liquids and an ecosystem of microbial life, small creatures and plant roots. One gram of soil might have between 50,000 to 1 million different species in it!

The composition and properties of soil can vary greatly depending on the following:

- the parent material (underlying geological material)
- the original rock minerals
- the particle size (clay, silt, sand), which determines the soil's texture
- the types of life that inhabit the soil.

Soil texture

The particle size of the rocks that make up the soil has a major impact on the way that soils behave, and their ability to retain or drain water.

Clay is the smallest soil particle. Clay soils can retain a lot of water, but in doing so they become sticky and heavy. During heavy rain, dry clay tends to seal up and create a slippery membrane that prevents the soil from absorbing the water, which leads to flooding. This characteristic can help you recognise it. Wet clay soil will feel sticky and smooth in your hands.

At the other end of the scale, sand grains are the biggest soil particles. Sandy soils are so porous that water drains away through them very quickly and plants dry out. Sandy soil will feel crunchy and gritty in your hands when wet and crumbly when dry.

All soils comprise a combination of clay, silt and sand. Good vegetable-growing soil will have a balanced mixture of these elements, giving it the ability to retain water but not to get clogged. That sweet spot of soil texture is called loam, which is an even mixture of sand and silt, with a little clay present too.

Knowing your soil type will help you understand the strong points of your soil, and where you should concentrate your efforts to improve it.

Depending on the relative percentages of sand, clay and silt, your soil might be categorised as sandy loam, silt loam, silty clay and so on. Rather than focusing on the exact definition, the important thing here is to understand the general properties of your soil and how they affect your gardening.

Loamy soils are the best for gardens because of their ability to retain water and nutrients for the plants, yet drain well and not turn anaerobic (no oxygen present). However, bad farming practices can degrade, compact or reduce the organic matter in even the best loam soil, making it unviable. On the flip side, regardless of the type of soil you start with, soil can be built up, improved and flourish with the right practices, additional organic matter and mineral amendments.

The jar soil-texture test

This is a simple and relatively reliable way to identify your soil's texture profile at home. This test separates the soil into sand, silt and clay layers.

1. Go to a representative area of your garden, and with a trowel take about a cup of soil about 5 cm (2 inches) deep. If there is compost or mulch at the top of the soil, exclude them from the sample. We want to check the soil texture and not the organic matter.
2. Break up any clumps of soil.
3. Place the soil sample into a clear jar (500 ml (17 floz / 2 cups) or larger). Fill the jar close to the top with water, and shake for several minutes. Leave the jar to stand.
4. Within a minute, the sand particles will have settled. Depending on your soil, the sand can split into fine and coarse sand. Mark a line on the jar showing where the sand has settled.
5. Within an hour, mark where the silt layer has settled.
6. The clay layer can take a while longer to settle, even up to a few days. Once the water at the top is clear, you can mark the clay layer with confidence.

Now that the distinct layers within the soil are marked, you can measure the percentage of each layer as part of your soil. Use the following diagram to determine your soil's classification, by finding the point where the three percentage lines meet.

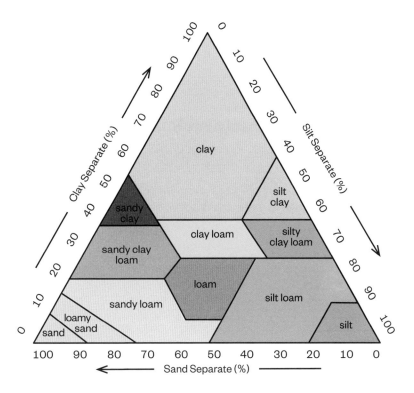

Soil can be separated into layers, which you can identify by texture and colour. The top layer, the topsoil, is our most valued treasure. Depending on the history of the soil and the bedrock it is made of, the topsoil layer can be very shallow (as little as a few centimetres), or it can be metres deep.

Building your topsoil

In nature, it takes a long time for topsoil to build up, but as a gardener, you can improve your topsoil's structure every season, making it optimal for plant growth.

You are striving to create deeply loose soil with good drainage, that feels crumbly, with a rich dark colour. An optimal soil has a high content of organic matter and is full of life, including a diverse range of microorganisms. Soil that maintains good moisture and nutrient-holding capacity and is well mineralised for the optimal health of our plants is ideal.

Although some soil characteristics can't be changed, other characteristics can be improved by:

- building and maintaining a healthy soil structure
- increasing soil organic matter
- cultivating a complex and abundant biological community
- creating optimal balance of minerals.

These elements of soil health are all interconnected. Although you can make large gains by working on each element separately, the combination of all four is the key to optimal soil health and plant health.

Increasing soil organic matter

Organic matter refers to plant, animal and microbial material, both living and dead, and it serves many critical functions in our soils.

Regenerative growing is about increasing the health of our ecosystem, not merely sustaining it. In vegetable gardens, this can be achieved by increasing the organic matter in the soil and building topsoil. Organic matter is one of the most important food sources for the creatures living in our soil. Feeding your soil's living community leads to improved plant nutrient absorption and soil structure.

The beautiful thing about adding organic matter is that it doesn't matter what type of soil you have; it can always be improved by adding organic matter. Organic matter is extremely beneficial for our regenerative growing system, as it improves the soil condition and leads to better plant growth. In clay- and silt-dominated soils, organic matter improves the drainage, air penetration, workability and aids faster warming of the soil in spring. In sand-dominated soils, organic matter helps to retain water and nutrients.

Organic matter helps plants to access a wider range of nutrients regardless of your soil's pH, whether it be acidic or alkaline. It will help balance the soil to the optimal levels for growing vegetables, which is 6–6.5 on the pH scale. We explain later in this chapter how to test your soil's pH.

You can increase the organic matter in your soils through particular gardening methods. Healthy plants usually have more than half of their biomass embedded in their roots. Therefore, leaving the roots of plants in the soil as much as possible, when weeding or clearing a bed, allows them to decompose in situ.

When we cultivate our soils, we aim to oxidise the soil as little as possible, which is one of the reasons we don't dig or rototill our garden beds. (Rototilling is the process of using tines that rotate quickly and deeply.) Every time the soil is tilled, it gets oxidised. In the short term, this makes the organic matter more available to the soil life, but over time this oxidising depletes the soil's carbon bank.

Additionally, there are many ways to incorporate organic matter into the soil. These include incorporating compost, vermicast (worm droppings), woodchips, straw or leaf mould mulch, and activated charcoal (biochar). When bringing in materials, always make sure that they are free from weed seeds.

It is important to integrate organic matter in its appropriate state. For high-carbon organic mulches, such as straw, woodchips and sawdust, this means using them after they have had time to break down for at least several months, otherwise they might deprive your crops of nitrogen. For compost, it means that the decomposition has been completed, and the compost has been properly cured, as we will discuss in chapter 11. For biochar, it means that the charcoal has been embedded in and interacted with organic matter prior to been added to the garden.

Cultivating a complex and abundant biological community

The regenerative approach to growing healthy plants relies on a healthy soil's biological community. Healthy soils have an abundant and diverse biological community, consisting of bacteria, fungi, protozoa, nematodes and arthropods.

Due to different disturbances to the soil, such as tilling and the

Below Forking in bed using a wide garden fork.

use of chemicals in agriculture, these life forms, and the food web that relies on them, are no longer present in all soils. This has huge implications, as these microscopic life forms fulfil many critical roles in building and maintaining healthy soils, as well as feeding our plants.

Plants have developed symbiotic relationships with soil microbes and mycorrhizal fungi over millions of years of evolution. As plants photosynthesise, they use the sun's energy to convert water and carbon dioxide into carbohydrates such as sugar. Plants are designed to support soil health, so much that up to 40 per cent of the total carbohydrates they make are released into the soil to feed the microbial community.

The root's exudate is a mixture of substances secreted by its root systems to feed microorganisms and deter pathogens. The exudate can include sugars, amino acids, organic acids, nucleotides, flavonoids, antimicrobial compounds and enzymes.

This mixture is different for each plant and is the basis of the specific plant–microbe symbiotic relationship. This activity happens in the rhizosphere (the soil zone surrounding the plant roots), which includes the chemicals and the microbiological community that are influenced by the roots.

This feed is reciprocated when, in simplified terms, these microorganisms convert the organic matter in the soil and even break down rocks, pebbles and soil particles (clay, sand and silt), and make the nutrients and minerals available to the plants. Win-win.

To provide full nourishment to your plants, it is critical that both decomposers (bacteria, fungi, nematodes) and predatory microorganisms (nematodes, protozoa, arthropods) are found in the soil, and are in balanced proportions to each other. This provides a safe habitat so that complex interactions can take place. Although it sounds a bit complicated, it is quite simple to accomplish, as we describe below.

Bacteria and fungi also affect the soil structure by forming aggregates, composed of microorganisms, organic matter and soil particles. These aggregates create pores that hold air and water, and also keep the soil intact and therefore less prone to erosion. Larger living organisms in the soil, which feed on microscopic life forms and organic matter, make tunnels that create further space for air and water and allow easier penetration of plants' roots deeper into the soil.

Cultivating the living community in your soil

Soil microbes love plants. So as much as possible, *try to keep your gardens filled with as many plants as you can fit in a bed without losing productivity*, and for as many days of the year as possible.

The next best thing is to *incorporate organic matter on the top of your soil*. The majority of the roots and microbes are concentrated at the top 10 cm (4 inches) of the soil's profile, the rhizosphere, and that is where you want to add your organic matter. Although some gardeners prefer to use compost as mulch, we think compost has a better outcome when it is shallowly integrated into the soil, using a rake.

Integrate compost into the soil a few times during the season rather than spreading your yearly supply all at once. Would you want to have a year's worth of food given to you all in one go? In nature, organic matter gets dropped onto the surface regularly. Feeding organic matter to the soil's microorganisms in small amounts helps keep their population in balance.

Keep your soil's structure intact to protect your living soil. Because different soil creatures live in different layers, it's best not to invert or mix these layers together as this will cause habitat disturbances that will stress the microorganisms.

Keep your soil moist to provide the best conditions for microorganisms. As the soil dries up, it stresses the soil's living community, which then either hibernates or dies as a result. Mulching refers to covering the soil with plants. Plants can also act as mulch, and are referred to as 'living mulch'. Other forms of mulching include dry plant material such as woodchips and straw, or artificial material such as weedmat. *Mulching your soil* is important to create a stable environment for the soil's living community to flourish in. One of the main advantages of mulch is that it protects the soil from dehydrating and therefore helps retain moisture, which is key for all living things to thrive.

Introduce beneficial bacteria into the garden by inoculating the soil. Providing good-quality organic matter inputs and providing microbes with what they need to thrive will help the living community to grow. But that may not be enough, and *inoculation with beneficial microbes can help you to build a complex biological community.* Inoculation can be with high-quality compost, or liquid sprays such as compost teas (we explain how to make them in chapter 11), raw milk, fermented liquids and bio-fertilisers. Some companies sell biological inoculants in powder form, which you can sprinkle directly onto your soil or seedlings or mix with molasses and lukewarm water to spray on the soil and plants.

Lastly, don't apply chemical fertilisers, fungicides or pesticides that will compromise soil biology.

Mineral balancing strategies

Plants, like all living creatures, need a broad range of elements to be able to function properly. When an essential mineral is missing or is not available in the amount needed by the plant, it becomes a limiting factor to plant health and productivity.

Minerals are needed in different quantities, and they are all connected to each other. The ratios between them are just as important as their presence or absence in our soils.

We only use natural soil amendments, which are described below. *Chemical soil amendments, which are commonly used in the farming industry, destroy the soil biology, are an environmental hazard, and are prohibited by organic certification agencies.*

To test or not to test

The more you know about your soil, the more tools you will have to amend and improve it. Laboratory and DIY mineral-testing kits can give you insights into your soil's mineral composition, which can help determine what fertilisers are best in your situation.

You can easily test your soil's pH at home with an inexpensive soil pH metre or litmus paper. To test with litmus paper, use a

Essential minerals for plant growth

There is a debate in the scientific community regarding which minerals plants need, in what form, in which quantities, and in what ratios. Seventeen minerals have so far been identified as absolutely essential for plant growth. Without them being present in sufficient quantities, deficiencies can be observed on plant leaves and growing habits. These are carbon (C), hydrogen (H), oxygen (O), nitrogen (N), phosphorus (P), potassium (K), sulphur (S), calcium (Ca), magnesium (Mg), iron (Fe), boron (B), manganese (Mn), copper (Cu), zinc (Zn), molybdenum (Mo), nickel (Ni) and chlorine (Cl).

trowel to dig a small handful of soil from about 10 cm (4 inches) deep. Mix the soil with twice the amount of distilled water, dip in the litmus paper and compare the colour to the pH index that came with the paper.

If you are growing in a small garden or on a short-term rental property, purchasing a bag of broad-spectrum organic fertiliser is a good way to go, instead of spending money on soil testing. While the fertiliser won't be exactly tailored to your soil's needs, it will still increase the amount of deficient minerals and will lead to improved growth. If the pH of your soil is not alkaline, adding lime can be another good alternative. With the low cost per square metre (10.7 square feet), around $1 to $3 annually, it is well worth the investment.

If you are growing a substantial-sized garden and will be gardening in it for the long term, you can look at investing in a soil test and a custom fertiliser mix for your soil. Consider engaging a consultant or fertiliser company that specialises in nutrient density and biological farming. They can help you to choose the right soil tests, explain how to interpret them, and create a fertiliser application plan that suits your specific conditions.

Crushed rocks

Rock fertilisers, such as crushed rock phosphate, volcanic rock, granite, gypsum and limestone, are a great way to add minerals to your soil, unlike synthetic minerals that damage the soil's biological community. Of course, there can always be too much of a good thing, so light spreading is always recommended. We suggest spreading about a handful (150 to 200g) per square metre (10.7 square feet), before planting or up to four times a year.

The effects of rock fertilisers incorporated into the soil are usually not immediate, but their benefits will carry on for much longer than the current growing year. In a home garden, where the soil biology is activated and thriving, and organic matter is composted or mulched back into the soil, solid fertilisers are mostly needed in the first few seasons and much less as the garden matures. Lime and gypsum are the most common solid fertilisers used in gardens, because they contain calcium, an important element for the garden that is often depleted. Unless your soil's pH is alkaline, adding lime will usually benefit your soil. Rock phosphate is another all-rounder rock fertiliser, composed of phosphorus (P) and calcium (Ca), which most gardens will benefit from incorporating.

Most companies that sell solid organic fertilisers base their products on crushed rocks, and there are many generic organic fertilisers blends that you can use. Unfortunately, the organic trademark is not enough to guarantee the sustainable and ethical sourcing of manufactured products. We suggest calling the fertiliser company to ask about where they source their ingredients from and to look for organic, locally sourced fertilisers or rock dusts that are the by-products of other operations.

Growing cover crops to accumulate certain minerals and bring them into the topsoil is another excellent strategy, which we will explore in chapter 9.

Right Yotam using a wide bed preparation rake.

Chapter 3
Starting a new garden

Let's now look at how to establish a vegetable garden. We will show you three different styles of garden beds, all of which are good options.

We like to say that gardening isn't cheese making; there isn't one method you need to strictly follow to make it work. Instead, use the principles we explain in this chapter to demystify what it takes to create a garden and then choose the best technique for your situation.

Establishing a new garden takes a bit of work, regardless of the garden-bed style you choose. To keep things fun and manageable, we highly recommend biting off only what you can comfortably chew. If all you think you can manage at the moment to establish and take care of is a 2 square metre bed (21.4 square feet), go for it! It doesn't have to be a perfect garden that lasts forever. If you feel like you need a bit of support, or you want to share this learning experience with friends, a great way to kickstart your new garden is to organise some snacks and invite a few friends over for a weekend gardening working bee.

Soil Profile

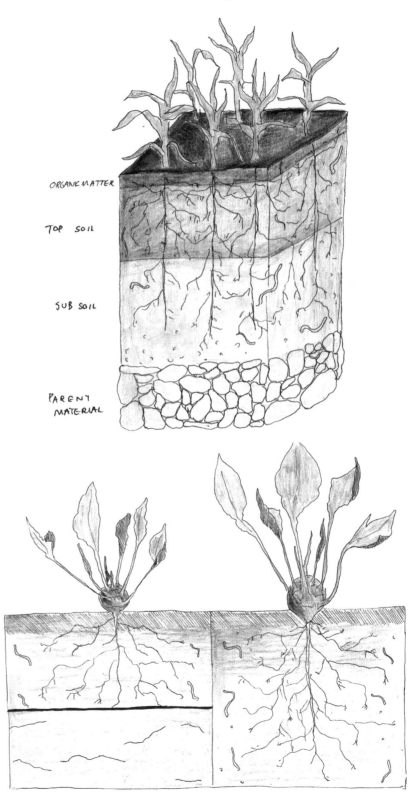

ORGANIC MATTER

TOP SOIL

SUB SOIL

PARENT
MATERIAL

Right Kohlrabi growing with a hardpan on the left, and kohlrabi growing without a hardpan on the right.

Building and maintaining a healthy soil structure

Once you have chosen your site, think about your soil. The way you prepare and maintain your growing beds will help to enhance the health and structure of your soil.

For the soil's biology to function properly, and for plant roots to be able to colonise the bed quickly, it is crucial to have sufficient air in the soil. The deeper that air can be brought into the soil, the deeper the biological community can thrive. A healthy soil structure has about 50 per cent of its volume in pores, or open space, which are usually half filled with gases and half with water. Once the soil has been loosened, you can try to avoid compacting the soil by keeping it covered with plants or mulch, and by not stepping on it.

An essential attribute of healthy soil is that it does not have a hardpan. What is a hardpan? It is a layer of soil, usually in the topsoil layer or just below it, that neither water nor plant roots can penetrate. Many things can cause a hardpan, and most soils have one to some degree. One of the causes of a hardpan is compaction by vehicle, human and animal traffic. It can also be caused by leaving the ground exposed for long periods, from chemical use, drought, improper watering and acidic soils.

Eliminating the hardpan in the vegetable garden is very important, as it allows you to cram many more plants into the same bed, increasing your yields dramatically.

There are two main strategies for breaking down a hardpan. The easiest method is a 'slowly but surely' approach, adding organic matter and allowing creatures such as earthworms and plant roots to break the hardpan for you over a few seasons. This can be achieved with or without supplemental forking.

The other option is more labour-intensive, and requires digging deep or forking and physically breaking the hardpan up. In severe hardpan cases, this is the only way to get rid of it. We find that as long as the topsoil layer is not mixed with the subsoil layer, making a mess in the topsoil layer to break up the hardpan does not cause any long-term damage.

When hardpan is found in acidic clay soils, whether it was caused naturally or not, adding a small amount of gypsum or lime

Above Earthworms decompose
organic matter and improve
the soil's structure.

can help to break up the hardpan and keep the soil loose.

When organic matter levels are high, and the soil's biological community is healthy, the soil's structure is typically good, too. Crumbly soil is an indicator of good soil structure, which is also characterised by fine aggregates with no significant soil clods, free-draining rather than puddles on the surface, and a sweet smell, which is a result of aerobic conditions.

As well as providing a great habitat for plants, healthy soil is resilient. It recovers well from disturbances such as extreme weather events, and is better able to withstand degradation and erosion.

Marking the garden

First, let's start by figuring out how your garden design translates to your site. Mark the garden perimeter and the width and length of your future garden beds with objects such as stakes, string, rocks or even liquid chalk.

With the visual representation of the garden laid out on the actual site, you can now 'try it out'. Walk on the paths you marked through the garden, pretend to be doing garden tasks and see how they feel. This is your opportunity to make any tweaks to the design. If you are not sure, just leave it for a few days. Make sure the garden makes sense, and the position and flow are good. Is it easy enough to navigate between beds? Is it comfortable to carry the harvest to the house from the various parts of the garden? Is there any shading that you did not expect over your growing area?

No-dig in-ground beds

We prefer no-dig in-ground beds and we have used this gardening technique when establishing our own gardens. This approach has many benefits as it requires no external inputs besides your labour, and it is fairly light work.

To make this system work, you do need some topsoil on your garden site. If you don't have at least 20 cm (8 inches) of

Right No-dig in-ground beds are created and maintained by forking.

Starting a new garden

topsoil, this might not be the system for you. Instead, look at framed raised beds or the lasagna-beds systems described later in this chapter as potential starting points. *If you do have topsoil, the no-dig in-ground system offers the highest return for the amount of energy invested than any other gardening method we know.* It involves simply eliminating any existing ground cover and forking to loosen up the soil.

Eliminating the existing ground cover

When we start a new garden, the first step is to remove the existing ground cover. Perennial vegetation such as a lawn or paddock must be completely dead before you start growing vegetables in that area. If not thoroughly eliminated, the grasses and weeds will regrow. It is very labour-intensive to remove this vegetation by hand, so it's therefore crucial to get rid of the perennial ground cover before starting to grow vegetables, and it makes it much easier to manage the garden weeds from that point.

Our preference is to cover the entire area with weedmat (woven landscaping fabric), tarps or a heavy layer of woodchips. Besides being very effective, earthworms thrive on the stable, moist environment under woodchips, tarps and weedmat.

The theory behind this method is that the vegetation will die out due to the lack of access to sunlight, coupled with the high temperature resulting from using weedmat and tarps. This process can take as little as a month in summer if the grass is kept short. Most grasses and plants will take two to three months to completely die, especially when the vegetation is high, and the plants have significant energy reserves. To assist this process, always mow the vegetation low before covering the area. Covering a wider area also helps get rid of tough grasses such as kikuyu and couch, as it deprives them of places to re-establish themselves.

When using weedmat or tarps, be sure to lay them out with adequate weights or pins, so they don't flap or fly away on a windy day. This also speeds up the process in the summer, as the heat 'bakes' the covered vegetation. If you are planning a fairly big

Sourcing organic matter

Think about where you are going to source organic matter for the garden. Using your own homemade compost is the ideal solution. Still, with the large amounts of compost needed in the first few seasons, you are likely to find yourself buying in compost. Look for locally made compost, made from organic ingredients. It is really important that your compost is clean from seeds and that it is appropriately aged. We will dive deeper into the art of composting in chapter 11.

We source our woodchip mulch from a local arborist, but you should easily be able to source it from a landscaping yard. Look for hardwood tree mulch, and try to avoid coniferous tree mulch, as it tends to have allelopathic properties (where one plant

The Abundant Garden

hinders the growth of another). If you are buying in straw, make sure it is organic and free of seeds. Non-organic straw may have been heavily sprayed and can contaminate your garden.

Leaf mould is created by the slow decomposition of leaves by various fungi, over one to two years, resulting in a great source of organic matter, though poor in nutrients. Leaves decompose best in a shady and moist environment, similar to the conditions under a forest floor.

Biochar is charcoal created in high temperatures and then inoculated. It lasts in the soil for centuries, unlike compost and mulches, which disappear in a season. When prepared properly, it acts as a great microbial additive. You can learn how to make your own biochar in small or large amounts. If you buy biochar, make sure it is locally and properly made.

garden and have a limited amount of covers available, you can do this section by section. As you move the covers from one area to the next, your newly uncovered section can be turned into garden beds and planted with crops.

When applying woodchips, a thick layer of at least 20 cm (6 inches) is needed to suppress the existing vegetation. Placing a layer of cardboard on the ground before covering it with woodchips can help with this process. If any weeds do pop up, make sure to pull them out as early as possible.

Chickens can do a great job of clearing an area by eating and scratching the existing vegetation. If you decide to fence an area for them to clear, you should still let them graze outside this area for a few hours a day. Otherwise, it is best to bring them fresh vegetation to eat, in addition to their regular feed, so that they continue to have a healthy diet while finishing the job of clearing your new garden area.

If you are in a hurry to get started, you can dig and remove the top 5 cm (2 inches) of soil, including all the vegetation. This soil is the most fertile part of your topsoil, so don't throw it away; instead, pile it up and cover it with a tarp. Once the vegetation dies off, you can incorporate it back into your garden beds. You could also loosen the ground and pull out the weeds one by one, but we'd much prefer to use time as our ally and avoid unnecessary work!

Forking, not digging

After removing the cover, or moving the woodchips to the side, it's time to mark the beds again. We use string and stakes to mark our beds and paths, to help us keep all the beds lined up and the same width. It is helpful to tie the string on the stakes 30 cm (12 inches) or so above ground, so the strings are out of the way of forking.

Using a sturdy fork, push the fork into the ground, as deep as you can without using excessive force. Orienting the fork on a slight angle towards the bed will allow for better body alignment while forking. In rocky soils, wiggling the fork from side to side or front to back helps to pass it through the rocks.

Once the fork is in the ground, slightly pull the fork towards

Above Expanding the garden using weedmat to eliminate perennial vegetation.

you. You should be able to do this activity with a straight back and good posture. The movement of the fork in the ground is intended to loosen the soil without breaking the soil's structure.

When you encounter too much resistance from the soil, take the fork out and take another bite, 5 cm (2 inches) apart. Be gentle; you don't need to use excessive force. No need to break your fork or your back!

Go as deep as you can but don't worry if you can't get the fork all the way into the soil the first time you open up a new bed. With every growing season, as you add organic matter and keep the soil moist, the plants' roots will reach deeper and deeper, allowing you to reach greater forking depth. After a season or two, we prefer to use forks with long tines of about 30 cm (8 inches) in length to help us achieve greater depth in the soil.

Keeping your soil's structure intact is very important for building up the soil's living community. This is why the no-dig approach is so vital for ongoing soil health.

Forking the soil also introduces air to the soil microbes, without inverting the soil's layers. When digging and flipping the soil, the layers get mixed up, and the living community suffers a huge disturbance. Organic matter from the top is now found deep in the soil, where there isn't enough air for aerobic biological activity to break it down. Without enough oxygen, anaerobic digestion can occur, which produces methane gas, as well as hydrogen sulphide, which smells like rotten eggs. The organic matter ends up turning into a sludge-like material that is harder to further decompose.

When working in compacted soil, the key is to 'bite' into the soil with the fork in small chunks, taking a new bite every 5–10 cm (2–4 inches). Pull the fork backwards towards you so there is less resistance to the forking action when every bite is going into the already loosened ground. Forking this way doesn't only make it easier to do with less effort, it also helps break the soil into small pieces, avoiding large clumps. With every consecutive bed forking between crops, you will eventually be able to increase the gap between bites to every 30 cm (12 inches) or so. Dig out any rocks you find, so eventually the growing bed will be only filled with usable topsoil. If you are working in a rocky area, it might take a few seasons to get rid of all these stones, so keep at it. In our

Right Garden bed forking sequence.

The Abundant Garden

INSERT FORK

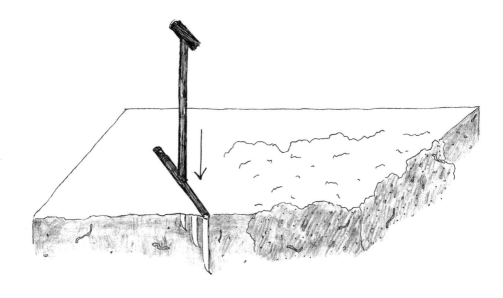

LEVER

ADVANCE BACKWARDS

rocky soil, we removed about 5 litres of rocks per square metre (10.7 square feet) of garden!

When working with silt or clay soils, the soil needs to be moist to be able to fork it. If the ground is too dry, give it a good soak and return to the task the next day.

Ideally, you will fork the garden bed as little as possible. Although it is a mild intervention to the soil's structure, it is still an intervention. Initially, it is highly beneficial to fork the bed between every crop, as it improves the depth of the topsoil and brings in air as the soil compacts. Once the soil's structure improves and the biological activity thrives, the soil needs less and less forking to maintain it.

Forking should be done in spring, to help boost soil life and recover from the compaction of winter rains. You can also fork the beds if the crop going in will benefit from it; for example, carrots and parsnips need the soil to be relatively loose to grow deep and straight.

The soil doesn't need to be super fluffy. In fact, we find that too much aeration can be a problem for healthy root growth, and that excessive drainage makes it harder to keep water in the soil. Our general rule is if the soil or the crop doesn't need it, we don't do it.

Amending the soil

Once you have completed forking your new garden bed, it is time to add compost. When the bed is first formed, a layer of 5 cm (2 inches) is a good start. The top 5–10 cm of the soil (2–4 inches) is where most soil life and plant roots are concentrated, so mix the compost shallowly with the top layer of the soil using a rake. You can sprinkle a handful of broad-spectrum natural fertiliser per square metre (10.7 square feet), either below or above the compost application. Just remember that it is much better to add small amounts often, rather than all in one hit.

Compost is a valuable resource that we want to use wisely. Most compost gets used up by the soil's biological community within three to six months, so it is better to spread it out in small amounts over the season. If you have a limited amount of compost, use it in thinner layers. Even if you have an ample supply available,

5 cm (2 inches) several times a year is plenty. There is a correlation between compost application and plant health and yield, but beyond a certain point, it stops making a difference. You would be better off spending your energy on other aspects of your garden.

We would only suggest adding more compost and mixing it deeply in very sandy or clay soils. Mixing the compost more deeply (up to 20 cm [8 inches] deep) will help to build a better soil structure. But generally, we prefer not to bury compost deep, because to decompose properly, it needs to be in an aerobic environment.

Shaping the beds

When organic matter has been added, and air pores increased due to forking, the height of the garden bed will rise. The amount the soil rises depends on the soil types. When we first established our beds, we shovelled soil from the path onto the bed. We thought that the topsoil was wasted on the paths and that we would have better plant growth that way. Although that might be true, we found that our garden drained extremely well, and the edges of the beds kept drying out too quickly, compromising the plants'

Below Various bed shape styles.

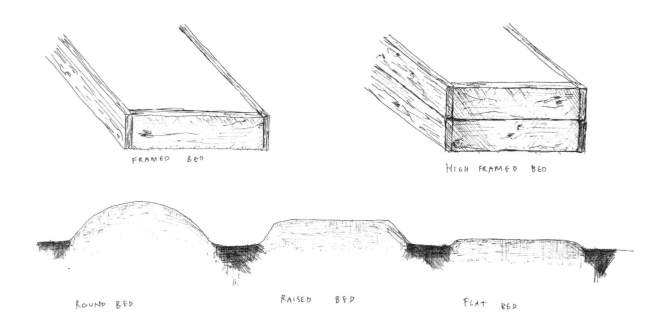

FRAMED BED

HIGH FRAMED BED

ROUND BED

RAISED BED

FLAT BED

health. Now we keep our garden beds only slightly raised, which occurs naturally from forking and adding organic matter.

If you are on a wet site and improved drainage would be beneficial, it is a good idea to raise your beds 5–15 cm (2–6 inches) above the level of the bed path. Raised beds warm up quickly as there is more surface area to capture the sun's rays. If you are on a dry site and water retention is your priority, then raised beds will have a negative effect. Flattening the beds close to ground level reduces evaporation and keeps the bed edges moist. Filling the paths with a heavy mulch layer in the spring can also help to prevent drying out.

Edging

The perimeter around the beds needs to be managed to prevent weeds from crawling back into the beds. Whatever you choose to do, it is a good idea to keep the vegetation close to the garden beds mowed short.

There are several ways you can go about forming an edge to your garden. You can form a narrow path around the beds and keep it weed-free with a hoe, or covered with cardboard and woodchips. Another option is to lay a permanent strip of weedmat or pavers around the edge of the garden, which will protect the ground and keep the edge maintenance free.

Framed raised beds

Raised beds can be built from a range of materials, depending on personal preference and what materials are available. The most commonly used materials are naturally rot-resistant wood, bricks, rocks and stabilised adobe. Raised beds can be as low as one 20 cm (8 inch) board or as high as 60 cm (24 inches) off the ground.

Raised beds are a good solution when the topsoil layer is very shallow or non-existent, or your ground is very rocky. Raised beds offer excellent drainage, and can be located on any surface, as long as the water has a way to drain out. If the frame is sturdy, it can

Above Tomatoes in stabilised adobe raised beds in Harry's garden.

Right Potatoes in Harry's garden.

also be used as a seat. The elderly and gardeners with disabilities often find raised beds more accessible and easier to work.

The main disadvantages to raised beds are that they require extra inputs and work to build and fill, and they need more watering and are quicker to dry out. You might have framing materials already or be able to build with second-hand materials or locally sourced timber. If not, the carbon footprint of your garden significantly increases when materials are newly purchased, as well as incurring the upfront costs of the materials. Unlike in-ground beds, which anyone can create with nothing but a tarp and a fork, it takes a bit of skill to build raised beds, which could be a barrier for some people. Topsoil, compost or any other materials you choose to use need to be brought in and filled into the framed beds. Depending on the size and depth of your beds, this can add up to a lot of material.

Starting a raised bed

Start by laying weedmat or tarps on the ground to suppress the vegetation that might be present on the site. This will ensure that nothing will pop up from the bottom of the bed to the surface.

Alternatively, place a thick layer of cardboard at the bottom and place your fill on top of that. The paths between the beds can be left covered in vegetation, or you could lay weedmat and cover it with woodchips or gravel.

Frame height and soil depth

The general rule of building raised beds is that the higher you build them, the thicker and sturdier the construction of the frame needs to be. Though 30 cm (12 inches) is enough topsoil for plant growth, a total of 40 cm (16 inches) of topsoil will offer your plants more rooting room. The existing topsoil on your site, if there is any, should be included in these numbers.

As you will need to do some forking maintenance inside the beds and add compost, it is a good idea to leave 5 –10 cm (2–4 inches) of space between the top of the sides of the raised bed and the soil, so the soil or compost won't fall out. After filling the bed for the first time, the soil will naturally compact down, so you can take that into account.

Drainage

To increase the drainage of your raised beds, it is a good idea to fork and loosen up the ground on which you are going to build them. If you are building low raised beds on soil, that is all you need to do. If you are building tall raised beds and the substrate on which you are going to build them does not drain well, you will need to prevent water from pooling at the bottom, as this will be harmful to your plants and soil life. You can do this by adding a layer of stones or large gravel at the bottom of the bed.

If you are placing your beds on concrete, place a layer of weedmat above the gravel layer to keep soil from clogging up the gravel drainage over time. Before filling the bed with soil, take a hose and soak the structure to see what happens. Make sure water can escape from the bottom or the sides; if it can't, add a drainage pipe for each bed.

Fill

You have several options when it comes to filling the bed. The obvious one is topsoil. Landscape suppliers often have topsoil available, which they can either deliver to you or you can take home on a trailer. We suggest looking for loamy soil from a non-sprayed area. If you are bringing in soil, why not bring in the best? Good soil will only need compost to be added at the top, like in-ground beds.

An alternative to topsoil is to buy in organic potting mix or organic vegetable-growing media, which is usually composed of compost, pumice, peat, coconut fibre and fertiliser. Although these materials are beneficial for plant growth and can replace soil as a growing media, they are not soil. Another disadvantage is that mined peat and imported coconut fibres are often included, so buying these products has negative environmental effects.

If you are building your raised bed on concrete or other artificial surfaces, introduce worms and other beneficial organisms into the bed right from the start. Once the beds are built and filled, treat them as soil-based beds. With careful forking and regular application of compost, you will soon have a thriving living soil system.

Lasagna beds

Another great method for creating no-dig beds is the 'lasagna' or sheet-mulching system. This involves spreading layers of different organic matter on top of each other, creating a thriving environment for growing vegetables. The height of the bed depends on the materials used, but this method often forms a shallow raised bed. It can be left un-edged, or you could frame it as we discussed in the section on raised beds.

The lasagna-bed system has significant benefits, as it can be used on top of any soil, regardless of the type of vegetation. In some variations, it can be planted immediately. It uses waste materials that can often be sourced for free, and prevents weeds in the soil from germinating. Vegetables thrive in this organic matter-rich environment, and the beds hold moisture really well.

There are also a few disadvantages to this system. It takes time to organise, collect, store and spread the materials. While the materials are at the early stage of decomposition, they can attract pests such as rodents and slugs, providing them with a breeding ground. Dogs can also be attracted to it, which can make quite a mess. If you are building your beds on top of very persistent perennial weeds such as kikuyu or couch grass, a thick layer is needed to suppress them.

There are many variations of lasagna garden beds. The guiding principle is to alternate layers of carbon-rich materials with layers of nitrogen-rich materials. Some variations include compost and topsoil.

Building a bed this way is a bit like building a compost pile, and the beds can be done at any scale. The simplest variation is a layer of compost on the ground, a layer of overlapping thick cardboard, and another layer of compost. The advantage of using compost rather than topsoil is that it is much lighter and easier to handle, and that good compost is free from weeds. The advantage of using topsoil rather than compost, is that topsoil is more balanced and better suited to plant growth.

To make this technique work best, mow the vegetation and give the soil a good soak, as well as the cardboard layers.

Carbon-rich materials you can use include: cardboard, newspaper, woodchips, shredded paper, leaves, straw, sawdust, hay

Right Example of layering materials for creating a lasagna bed for immediate planting.

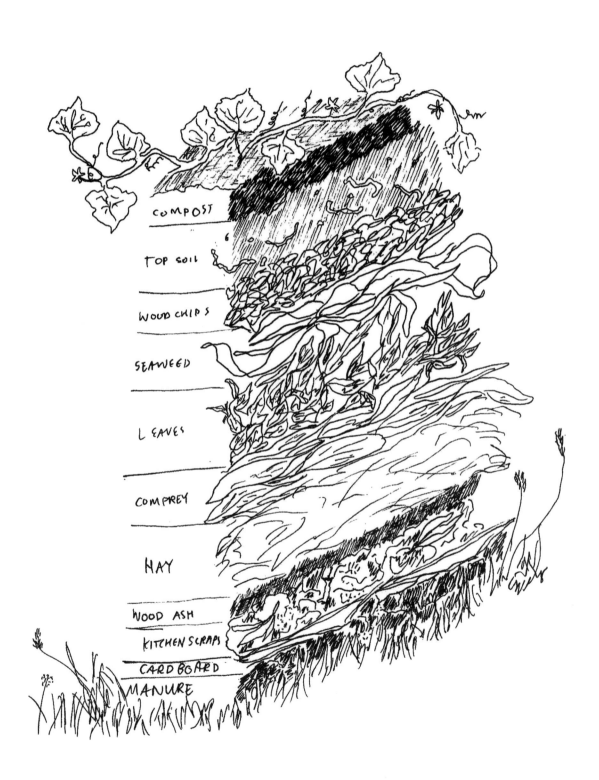

COMPOST

TOP SOIL

WOOD CHIPS

SEAWEED

LEAVES

COMPREY

HAY

WOOD ASH

KITCHEN SCRAPS

CARDBOARD

MANURE

(has heaps of seeds in it, so only use at the bottom of the layers), spoiled hay and dry plants.

Nitrogen-rich materials you can use include: kitchen scraps, seaweed, manure (use at the bottom of the layers for food safety if you plan to plant within a few months), weeds and green plant material, comfrey leaves, coffee grounds, grass clippings (if they have seeds then place them at the bottom).

Other beneficial ingredients you can add between the layers: rock fertiliser, wood ash and eggshells.

When layering, aim for the ratio of a double layer of carbon material for one layer of a nitrogen material. You don't need to be precise. Layers can be at any depth, and you can build the bed to whatever height you prefer. Finish off with a carbon layer to reduce any potential smell. If you wish to plant into this bed immediately, use compost, topsoil or a mixture of both.

For the decomposition to be possible, the bed needs to be kept moist, so make sure to give it a weekly watering if the weather is dry. If you are building your lasagna bed with no compost or topsoil, you will need to wait three to four months before planting.

Lasagna beds are best prepared in the autumn when there are lots of leaves around, in order to be ready for a spring planting. Since winter is often fairly wet, covering the bed with a tarp will prevent it from becoming anaerobic and leaching nutrients in the ground.

For immediate planting, layers could include: (bottom to top) kitchen scraps, cardboard, wood ash, comfrey and hay, leaves, seaweed, topsoil, woodchips, compost/soil/fertiliser mix.

If you don't mind waiting for three to four months before planting, layers could include: (bottom to top) manure, cardboard, kitchen scraps, leaves, manure, leaves, seaweed and woodchips.

After the beds are formed, treat them like you would any other garden bed.

Another variation of the lasagna-style method is a traditional European technique called Hügelkultur, in which small logs or branches are used as the first layer. The wood acts as a very long-term carbon source. These beds are usually quite tall and are shaped like a mound.

Starting a new garden

Chapter 4
Plant propagation techniques and planting in the garden

The magical process of growing plants gives us lots of satisfaction and is a big part of why we love gardening as much as we do. Seeds are just waiting for the cue to start growing.

Once out of the packet, seeds respond to changing conditions; the right temperature, humidity and a bit of sun tell them it is time to grow. The beauty of gardening is that plants want to grow, and you are simply assisting them by providing the best conditions you can to help them thrive.

Propagating is the process of growing plants from seeds, cuttings or other plant parts. Propagating your own plants has many advantages. It allows you greater freedom in choosing varieties, greater control over seedling quality, it is a lot more cost-effective than buying seedlings, and it allows you to take care of the plants from seed to harvest. Growing your own plants is relatively simple, but it requires regular attention, as we will explain in detail in this chapter.

Tips on purchasing seedlings

High-quality seedlings are the basis of a productive garden. While some nurseries and plant dispensaries will only sell healthy seedlings, others will sell plants that are past or before their optimal planting size so they can get rid of stock or because they are short of suitable plants. For the best results, take the following points into account when purchasing seedlings.

Seedlings should display growth that is proportionate to the size of their plugs. (A plug is a small seedling grown in seed trays filled with potting mix.) If the foliage of the plant is very large compared to the plug size, the plant's roots will not be able to support the plant well. Very small seedlings, with only one to two true leaves, might not be ready to go into the garden for a few more weeks.

Plants that have been sitting in their tray for too long will develop 'bound' roots. This appears as a thick root mass that covers the plug. Plants transplanted with bound roots tend to suffer from transplanting shock, and sometimes never recover. Gentle rubbing and disrupting these roots can invigorate these plants and lead to better growth, as it indicates to them that they are in a new environment.

Seedlings become pale

and leggy if they have been exposed to low amounts of light and will not result in a healthy plant.

Seedlings should have been hardened off (gradually acclimatised to an outside environment); check this with your vendor.

Purchasing organic seedlings means the potting mix is organic too. Non-organic potting mixes often contains fungicides and chemical fertilisers, as well as other contaminants from non-organic compost. If regularly used, these contaminants can have a negative effect on your organic garden.

Plants that are about to flower while in their tray or pot are past their best planting date, and should be avoided. If you want to give them a try, remove the flowering buds so that the plants can concentrate on growth.

Whether you are an experienced gardener or just starting on your gardening journey, you don't have to grow your own seedlings. Buying seedlings is an easy and sure way to have a garden full of vegetables. Most communities have an organic nursery selling healthy vegetable seedlings. Purchasing seedlings on a regular basis is a great way to have a reliable source of seedlings, as well as supporting a local business. Also, you can often pre-order your favourite seasonal varieties.

Once you have created your garden bed, or harvested a previous crop, you now have space available. It's wise to sow or plant it promptly. The soil needs protection, and Mother Nature will soon encourage the seeds that are already in the soil (also known as weeds) to germinate and cover the ground. So give your plants a better start by not procrastinating and fill in that clear soil quickly. If you're not going to use that space within a few weeks, it would be best to cover the bed with a tarp, weedmat or mulch to protect the soil and prevent the weeds taking over.

Propagation basics

Vegetable plants are generally divided into two categories: plants that are directly sown into the garden bed, and plants that grow as seedlings in trays, and are later transplanted into the garden. Each technique has its benefits, and you might choose one or the other depending on the crop and your gardening situation.

As we explain in depth later in this book, the same vegetable can be grown in several different ways and be harvested at different stages of its life. Therefore, depending on your culinary and gardening preferences, you might choose to direct sow beets, for example, or to transplant them as seedlings. Both options are totally acceptable, and personally, we move between them depending on our preferences at the time.

Direct seeding

We generally choose to direct sow plants for two main reasons. We direct sow plants that are grown for their edible roots, such as carrots, to let their taproots spread down without disturbance. The transplanting process can easily interfere with the roots' natural growing, so direct sowing is a safer method for root vegetables. All vegetable plants send out a main root, referred to as a taproot, which anchors the plant and is meant to go directly down and deep. When plants stay in their pots for too long, their roots get deformed, and although this won't stop them from growing, it will affect the structure of the roots and their health.

Another reason to direct sow is to grow quick-growing plants at a high density, such as radishes and mustard greens. Direct seeding saves time, is more cost-effective and requires less work to sow a patch compared to planting. When sowing leafy greens, radishes and carrots, you can sow them very densely, as much as 200 plants in a square metre. Direct sowing a large amount of plants takes a few minutes whereas planting can take a good hour.

How to direct sow in the garden

There are several techniques for sowing crops. For all techniques, it is essential that the soil stays moist. If the little germinating seeds dry out while they only have a tiny root, they will die.

The depth of sowing the seeds is determined by the size of the seeds, your soil's texture and the time of year. We have found that the common rule of thumb of sowing to the depth of double the seed's size is not completely accurate, although it is generally true that the smaller the seeds, the shallower they should be sown. Reducing the amount of soil tiny seeds have to pass through on their way to the open air and sunlight makes sense. The soil texture also plays a part; it is much easier for seeds to come through in sandy soils compared to clay soils.

It is possible to direct sow plants throughout the year, although some plants do much better at specific times in the year. Each season presents its own set of challenges. In the summer, plants grow quickly, but the soil needs to be kept moist by frequent watering. To compensate for this, in summer we aim to sow the

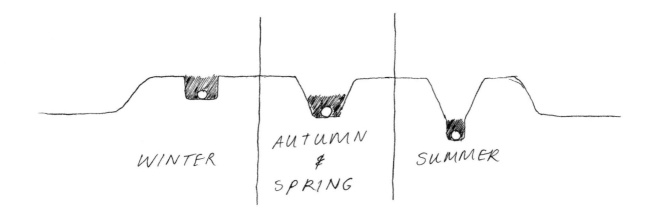

WINTER

AUTUMN & SPRING

SUMMER

Above Depth of sowing according to the time of year.

seeds deeper into the soil where moisture is more constant. In spring and autumn, natural rainfall is usually enough. Still, danger is lurking around the corner, as slugs enjoy the wet weather, as well as rodents and birds, and seek out the germinating seeds as their natural food sources are lower at this time. In the winter, the cold and wet weather will often create unsuitable sowing conditions unless the seeds are covered.

Sowing in a shallow furrow

Make a series of shallow furrows (long, narrow trenches in the ground) along the bed's width, if you want short rows, or the bed's length, for long rows. In the furrows, carefully sprinkle the seeds to your preferred density. Sprinkling the seeds at the right spacing takes a few goes to get right, but can be mastered quickly. A really good way to learn what works best for you is to measure with a measuring teaspoon how many seeds you have spread over a metre. Try a slightly different amount of seed in each furrow and record it in your gardening diary. At harvest, you can assess which density worked best, and use that as your guideline the next time you sow. We prefer to work with narrow furrows and have more of them, but we have seen gardeners successfully sow into wide furrows. Your garden is your playground, and you choose how to play.

A very common mistake is to space the seeds too close together, which leads to stunted growth. To avoid spreading the seeds too close, scatter them very lightly, and then repeat if needed. In general, the closer the seeds are to one another, the further apart the rows should be. Determining how many furrows per bed and what distance to space them depends on the vegetable variety, the density inside the row, and the size at which you want to harvest your crop.

In summer, it is better to create wider furrows about 5–7.5 cm (2–3 inches) deep. This helps to keep the seeds in an environment that is more consistently moist.

Here's a great tip to make this system work really well. Once you have sown your seeds in the furrow, cover them up with compost rather than topsoil. Using compost has several advantages. It makes the furrow very visible, but more importantly, if the compost is free of weeds (as it should be), only your seeded veggies will come up, and they will have far fewer weeds to compete with. It will also be easier to know which germinating seeds are the ones you sowed, and which ones are weeds. Another advantage is that the compost's dark colour will get warmer than the surrounding topsoil and will help the seeds to germinate faster.

Above Using the EarthWay seeder.

Below Quick growing radishes are direct sown in high density.

One seed at a time

In this method, instead of sprinkling the seeds, each seed is pushed into the ground at the appropriate spacings and depth. This technique is definitely more time consuming than sowing in a furrow, but it is significantly quicker than planting seedlings. Though it is generally more suitable for larger seeds, such as beans, radishes and pumpkins, it can also be done with smaller seeds such as lettuces and carrots. When using good seed and sowing under optimal conditions, the accurate spacing will reward you with very healthy plant growth. During the spring and early summer, direct sow the bigger seeds in a deep dimple, to funnel more water to the seed.

Scatter sowing over the bed

In this method, the seeds are scattered as evenly as possible across the bed and gently raked in with the soil. This method works best when there is very low weed pressure in the bed, as it can be quite difficult to distinguish between weeds and germinating vegetables.

To use this method, it is best to know how many seeds you have and how many you are aiming to scatter over a square metre. Always start with half the amount of seed you want to use, as the most common mistake using this method is to spread the amount of seed you need for the whole area on just half of it!

Most seed packets will mention how many seeds they contain. Just like we mentioned in the furrow method, it's best to experiment and record the results both at sowing time, and over the season or at harvest. By being systematic, learning from previous experiments and continually refining, you will significantly improve your gardening skills and yield.

Using a precision seeder

If you have a large vegetable garden, and you frequently directly sow large areas, you might benefit from using a precision seeder.

A precision seeder allows you to quickly drop seeds at exact spacings. Also, you can comfortably walk with a straight back while sowing the bed. Most seeders will make a small furrow, drop the seed, cover the soil and slightly firm it as they pass. Most seeders need relatively flat and even bed conditions to work well.

Two affordable precision seeders are the EarthWay and the Glaser seeders. The EarthWay uses interchangeable plates that can accommodate most seed sizes, and the furrow settings allow you to determine the depth your seeds will drop. The Glaser only sows small seeds well, and it is a bit fiddlier to work with, but it works much better for framed beds due to its small size and greater manoeuvrability.

Growing seedlings

It's simple to grow your own seedlings, and you don't need a fancy set-up. Any sunny benchtop, a bit of floor space in your home, or an outdoor bench can do the trick. Growing your own seedlings requires more effort than direct seeding because of the extra steps involved, but there are many reasons to do so.

- *Growing plants in trays allow you to fit another crop in the ground at the same time the seedlings are growing.* For example, when propagating lettuce seedlings in large cells, this allows you to grow the lettuces in the tray until the plants are five to six weeks old. In the meanwhile, the garden space can be occupied by a different crop, making your garden space go much further.
- *When planting healthy seedlings, it is more likely that every plant will survive.* This also helps us ensure optimal spacing between plants. When direct seeding, there would be more gaps, since not all of the seeds will germinate and make it to maturity.
- *Transplanting makes weeding easier.* If seedlings are planted at an advanced stage and grow quickly, you may not need to weed the bed at all between planting and harvest.
- You can fit many plants in a standard-sized tray, sometimes a full bed's worth. Instead of needing to keep the whole garden bed moist through the sensitive germination and seedling stage, you only need to keep the tray moist, which *saves you both water and time.*
- Starting plants from seeds allows you to grow them in a protected environment and gives you a head start of several weeks before conditions are ready in the garden. For example, we usually start our tomato seedlings 6–8 weeks before the last frost of the season. Once the frost danger is over, planting these mature seedlings will *reward us with an earlier harvest.*

Your aim is to grow seedlings with optimal nourishment and biological activity in their trays, so that they thrive in the garden and experience uninterrupted growth.

Making your own potting mix

Making your own potting mix is fun and rewarding. There are numerous ingredients you can use, though the most common and sustainable ingredients are your topsoil, compost, pumice and sand.

Topsoil can be 25–50 per cent to 50 per cent of the mix, depending on your soil's texture and workability. The sandier and siltier your soil, the more topsoil you can use. Compost can also be up to 50 per cent of the mix, and it can be either compost you make or buy. It is very important that your compost is well balanced and fully mature. Pass both your topsoil and the compost through a screen to break and remove large particles. To help remove any weed seeds in the compost and topsoil, spread a 5 cm (2 inch) layer over a tarp and keep it moist for about two weeks. During that time, seeds will germinate; you can get rid of them by either covering again with the tarp and preventing light for another week, or by exposing it to the sun without watering.

As composts are made from a wide range of ingredients, the quality and origin of the materials in the compost will significantly affect the quality of the potting mix.

Adding as much as 25 per cent small-sized pumice rock (a naturally occurring volcanic rock with lots of gas bubbles) would be extremely helpful in assisting with drainage, moisture retention, gas exchange and improving the soil's structure. Once planted, pumice stays in the soil, helping to improve the soil's structure and to release nutrients.

Coarse river sand can also achieve this, but sand is generally heavier and tends to compact more easily. Using up to 10 per cent sand in your potting mix could be beneficial.

Although peat moss, coconut fibre, vermiculite and perlite provide horticultural advantages, we prefer to avoid them because of their heavy ecological footprint.

To improve the potting mix's available nutrition and biological activity, it is beneficial to add natural fertilisers such broad-spectrum rock fertilisers and biological additives, and also biochar and seaweed (if available).

Growing medium

A good growing medium needs to be able to hold moisture, but at the same time provide sufficient drainage, so conditions stay aerobic. It also has to be fully mature, free from plant pathogens, clean of weed seeds and ideally biologically active. A good potting mix will have enough nutrients to keep the seedlings healthy right up until the transplanting stage, and ideally should have a good mineral balance. Unfortunately, even buying a premium organic potting mix doesn't guarantee all these things.

Tips for using potting mix:

- Use a premium potting mix or make your own (see sidebar) and keep it dry and in the shade until it needs to be used. If you buy bagged potting mix, wear a face mask when handling it to minimise the risk of contracting Legionnaires' disease, a type of pneumonia (lung inflammation) caused by exposure to a bacterium known as *Legionella*.
- We always mix a broad-spectrum solid fertiliser with our potting mix before using it. Add about 1 cup of broad-spectrum biologically inoculated fertiliser per 15 litres (4 gallons) of potting mix.
- Sow seeds into moist potting mix and keep the trays well-watered, by gentle watering from above with a hose, watering can or a sprayer. The trays should never dry out, especially at the germination stage. You can slow the soil from drying out by placing the seedling trays under a bit of shade and protecting them from winds. As the seedlings emerge, they need to be moved to full sunlight; otherwise they grow a long, thin stem, and become what is known as 'leggy'. You are after stocky plants with a short, sturdy stem. Another way to keep your tray moist is to place the seedling tray inside a shallow container filled with water. The water will soak up and keep the soil moist.

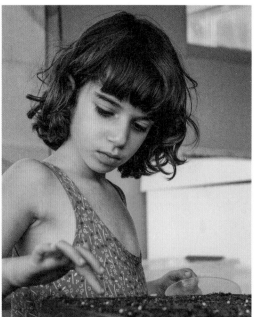

The Abundant Garden

Trays and pots

You can grow seedlings in many types of containers. Over the years, we have settled on the techniques that give us the most flexibility with the least work, while providing exceptional seedlings.

The first rule of plant propagation in containers is to be generous with the size of cells you are using and the spacing in between your seedlings. Any investment in your seedlings is an investment in your garden. You want balanced growth between each plant's foliage and its roots at planting time.

Different plants have different needs in terms of the size of pot they can grow in. Generally speaking, the bigger the plant will be at planting time and the longer the plants need to stay in the container, the larger the container needs to be.

You can use open trays or containers without dividers, or you can use pre-divided trays, commonly referred to as cell trays. Even small punnets, toilet roll inners and egg cartons can be used for propagation if you grow a relatively small number of seedlings.

Each type of container has advantages and disadvantages. Open trays allow you the most flexibility in terms of plant spacing, and the plants have a large area to draw nourishment from. You can build such trays from any source of untreated natural wood, even pallets, though if using hardwood they will last longer.

Cell trays are a mixed bunch, and we would recommend always using large cells, 5 to 6 cm (2 to 2.4 inches) wide, which can hold more nourishment and moisture than smaller cells.

The biggest advantage of cell trays over open trays is that plants can stay in them for longer. For example, lettuce sown in open trays needs to be planted in three to four weeks. If not, they can grow too big and don't transplant well. In the 5 cm (2 inch) wide cell trays, lettuces can keep healthy for up to five to six weeks. The extra two weeks gives us more time for other crops in the garden. More importantly, we can fit the planting into our busy schedule, as we enjoy a planting window of anywhere from three to six weeks from sowing.

You can sow several varieties of seeds in one tray, both in cell and open trays. When you do so, it is best to sow vegetables that take approximately a similar time to germinate and be ready for planting. For example, in one tray you could grow two rows of lettuce and one row each of broccoli, kale, spinach and zinnia.

Left above Starting and growing early season summer crops indoors.

Left below, left Lettuce seedlings in 5 cm (2 inch) cell tray.

Left below, right Lily sowing seeds in a tray.

Page 84 Cucumber seedlings in pots.

The Abundant Garden

Growing plants in sets

With some vegetables, you can grow sets of three to five seeds in the same cell that will be planted together, without being separated. The advantages of planting multiple seeds together and growing them all in one cell are as follows.

Space efficiency: You'll use fewer trays as more plants fit in the same container, which means using less space for propagation and less watering.

Time and energy efficiency: Planting a group of plants together means that instead of transplanting each plant individually, you only need one planting action for several plants.

Easier weeding: As the plant are organised in sets, but the number of plants per area is the same, there is a larger gap between plants, which makes weeding easier.

The main disadvantage of planting in sets is that sometimes it is harder to harvest a single plant from a set, so more plants have to be removed at the same time.

We grow the following plants in sets.

4–5 per set: spring onions, viola (for edible flowers), turnips, radishes and herbs.

3 per set: bulb onions, spinach and beets.

We usually use pots 8–10 cm (3.2–4 inches) wide to grow larger seeds and seedlings, such as cucumbers, courgettes and pumpkins, which are too big to fit in the 5 cm (2 inches) wide cells at three to four weeks. Placing a group of pots on a tray makes them easier to handle.

Sowing tips

First, fill your tray with your potting mix of choice, tap it a couple of times on the bench to let it settle, and top up with more potting mix so it is full to the brim.

If the quality of the seeds is good, and the seedlings are going to stay in their container for up to six weeks, plant each seed at the spacing you want it to be at planting time.

When the germination of the seeds is below 80 per cent (only eight of ten seeds germinate), or when there is large variability in the quality of the seeds, we suggest using a different technique. You can sow two seeds in the same cell, and if both germinated you can either thin out the weakest one or keep both of them and separate them at planting time into two transplants. Placing the seeds about 1 cm (0.4 inch) apart will make it easier to separate them if you chose to do so.

Another option is to sow the seeds close together, about 0.5 cm (0.2 inch) apart, in a group that will later be moved to another tray at a larger spacing, a practice known as pricking out.

Pricking out allows you to choose the best plants to continue growing, and you don't waste precious tray space in the meantime. Each seed is unique and grows a bit differently, something you will notice every time you germinate seeds. The seeds that germinate first, and grow the strongest, are the ones that have the most vigour and will likely grow into healthier, more productive plants. Choosing the best seedlings (and not pricking out or transplanting the weaker ones) is not a waste of seeds, but rather an investment in your garden, as it will help you keep your gardening space for high-yielding plants.

A couple of pricking-out tips:

- Pricking out the little seedlings at the cotyledon stage, before the plants develop their first set of true leaves, will lead to a better root structure.

Above and left Niva and Lily potting up eggplant seedlings from small cell trays into larger pots.

The Abundant Garden

- When handling little seedlings (and transplants), never hold them by their delicate stems as it will often stunt them or even kill them. Instead, handle plants by holding them by their leaves or roots.

When sowing seeds, it is always a good idea to label each tray or row with the name of the seed. Many things can be used for labelling: iceblock sticks, masking tape or a white permanent marker will all do the trick. Additionally, you can write down the vegetable variety, the sowing date, seed source and any other observations you make in your garden diary. It is helpful to review this information, especially when trialling different varieties and learning what works better for your garden situation and personal preferences.

Caring for your seedlings

Different vegetables each have their preferred temperature range for germinating (see the table overleaf). If conditions are too hot or too cold for their liking, germination will be low, or not happen at all.

After germination, the seedlings can handle a wider temperature range than they require during germination. Although their required temperature range can indicate what growing environment they prefer, and keeping the air and soil temperature to their liking will result in healthier plants.

Air circulation, ventilation and light are key factors in creating a healthy plant environment. The soil needs to be moist but not soggy to prevent it from being waterlogged, anaerobic and developing fungal diseases. Keep the growing environment sunny. If you are growing in a tunnel house, a small cloche or a germination box, keep the cover of your structure clean to allow adequate light exposure so your seedlings won't get leggy. If the seedlings are growing in an environment that is too hot, the foliage will grow out of balance in the tray without developing a suitable root structure; too cold, and the seedlings will be stressed and grow poorly.

Most vegetables have a wide temperature range in which they can germinate, so don't worry if your conditions are not ideal. Generally, the closer the temperature for the plants' comfort zone, the fewer days it will take to germinate, and the germination rate will also be higher.

This table is a guideline only, as different varieties within each vegetable have different germination rates and temperature preferences. It is the soil's temperature that counts and the soil temperature is usually significantly lower than the air temperature.

To help germinate vegetables that prefer the warmth, place their tray inside the house a few metres from the fireplace or in the hot-water cupboard, where temperatures are generally stable and warm. Water them with warm water, which will increase the potting mix's temperature without harming the plants. Once the plants emerge, move them outside where there is more sunlight, to avoid them getting leggy.

To grow stronger seedlings, you can apply a liquid fertiliser spray, a practice known as foliar feeding. There are many types of sprays you can use (as we discussed in chapter 2), which will provide the seedlings with additional nutrition and increase the biological activity for a better symbiotic relationship between plants and microbes.

For easy access, keep your foliar spray bottle in the shade, next to where you are growing your seedlings. These sprays are best used when they are diluted and applied often. Once every week or two is very beneficial.

Hardening off

Exposing the plants to the garden conditions several days before transplanting is called 'hardening off'. Plants prefer gradual change, so taking the plants outside will help them get used to the wind and sun before transplanting. The plants will respond by thickening their leaves, developing stronger stems and a thicker root mass. It's better to take plants outside for the first time when the day is overcast or in the evening, rather than on a stormy or very sunny day. However, if you are planting under the protection of a cloche, there is no need for hardening off.

While hardening off, it is always better to keep plants raised off the ground, to prevent them from rooting while in the trays.

Temperature range table for germination indoors and outdoors

Vegetable	Suitable soil temperature °C (°F) for germination	Number of days for seed to germinate
Basil	21–32 (70–90)	6–14
Bean (bush and climbing)	18–30 (65–86)	6–11
Beet (including chard)	12–26 (54–80)	6–12
Broad bean	10–21 (50–70)	6–10
Broccoli, cabbage and cauliflower	12–26 (54–80)	5–12
Capsicum	21–30 (70–86)	8–11
Carrots	12–30 (54–86)	8–21
Celery	12–24 (54–75)	9–14
Coriander	12–21 (54–70)	7–14
Corn	15–21 (60–70)	5–10
Courgette, cucumber	18–30 (65–86)	5–9
Eggplant	24–32 (75–90)	6–10
Endive	10–21 (50–70)	7–11
Fennel	10–21 (50–70)	9–14
Kale, kohlrabi	10–26 (50–80)	5–12
Leek, onion	10–26 (50–80)	8–14
Lettuce	10–26 (50–80)	5–10
Parsley	15–26 (60–80)	9–14
Parsnip	10–24 (50–75)	12–21
Pea	10–21 (50–70)	5–12
Pepper (chilli)	18–30 (65–86)	7–11
Pumpkin, squash, rock melon, watermelon	21–32 (70–90)	6–12
Radish, turnip	10–86 (50–86)	5–10
Rocket	7–18 (45–65)	4–8
Spinach	10–25 (50–80)	6–12
Tomato	15–30 (60–86)	5–10

Keeping them off the ground also helps to avoid pests such as slugs and mice, and to improve air circulation and drainage. The hardening-off area can be a sunny bench; if birds are eating your plants then placing a hoop or a cage with bird netting over them is essential. If your plants are growing too fast, you can slow their growth by moving the seedlings to the hardening-off area earlier.

When are the plants ready to go into the garden?

If the roots easily separate from the potting mix, it's better to leave them in the tray to harden off for a few more days. The potting mix should be held by a healthy root system that is not too bound and hard. It is best to plant the seedlings with as much root mass and potting mix as your plant has in its container, in order not to disturb the root system.

If the seedlings are root bound, gently disturb the root system to waken it up, so the plants will know that their environment has changed and that they should concentrate on new root growth. When your seedlings start shooting to the sky and even flower in their container, it means they have either been in the tray for too long or that they have been stressed. Sadly, they should be discarded rather than planted. It is possible to help plants recover, but they will never do as well in the garden, and it will be a waste of precious gardening space. One exception is tomato seedlings, which, once you remove the flowers, will continue to grow just as well as seedlings not left too long in the tray.

Pre-planting

The day before planting the seedlings in the garden, thoroughly water your seedlings. Soaking the plants or the whole tray in a tub with water and a bit of liquid fertiliser for a few minutes before planting helps to ensure that the root area of the plants is completely hydrated. The extra feed also helps plants recover from root disturbance faster.

Planting time

With enough care, your plants can be transplanted into the garden at any stage, and all plants can be grown by direct seeding in the garden if the conditions are right. The decision about when to plant them in the garden depends on how well you can take care of them, how close they are to overgrowing their container, and when the conditions are optimal. The smaller the plants, the more care

Above A simple propagation structure — wooden frame with hoops and a woven mesh cover.

Right Yotam with tomato seedlings in 10 cm pots.

The Abundant Garden

Plant propagation techniques and planting in the garden

you will need to give them in their first few weeks in the garden. The larger they are (up to a point), the hardier they will be. When transplanting overly large plants, remove a few of the lower leaves to create a more balanced plant, which will be easier for the root system to support while it is acclimatising to its new environment.

Planting on a cloudy or drizzly day helps prevent plants from drying out and reduces their stress. If there isn't a day when overcast weather is expected, it's better to plant early in the morning or, even better, late in the afternoon, rather than when the sun is at its strongest. Make sure to transplant into a well-hydrated bed and gently water the plants soon after planting.

Using the correct planting technique can make a massive difference to the health and yield of your plants. Seedlings of certain plants prefer to be planted at specific depths. The ideal planting depth can change according the conditions and the season.

- *At ground level.* Some plants prefer to be planted at the same ground level they germinated at. With these plants, the stem is sensitive and can easily be damaged, and it is essential not to apply pressure on it or bury it. This group includes most lettuces, cucumber, courgette, squash, fennel and sunflower.
- *Deeper than ground level.* Some plants benefit from being planted at a deeper level than they germinated at, usually up to the first true leaves. Planting this way helps the plants to support themselves physically without the need to invest unnecessary energy in developing a thick stem. There are many vegetables in this group, including tomatoes, eggplant, capsicum, kohlrabi, cabbage, kale, and broccoli. Tomatoes are a special case, as they can be planted much more deeply than other plants. We usually prune our 25 cm (10 inch) tall seedlings to leave only the top six leaves or so and then plant the stem about 10 cm (4 inches) deep.
- *Higher than ground level.* In some situations, it is beneficial to plant higher than ground level. This practice is more common in tree plantings or waterlogged soils, but we have also found that when growing winter lettuces where there is less chance of the plants drying out, it helps to plant them high, so there is better air circulation around the base of the plants.

In the home garden, when there isn't a large number of plants to transplant at any one time, it is worth being gentle with the seedlings. To transplant, move the soil to the side with your hand or a trowel, insert the plant at the correct depth, and fill in the gap. It's that easy!

Ensure the transplant potting mix is not exposed as it can dry out and stress your plants, and that seedlings have firm contact with the soil. With smaller seedlings, rain or overhead watering is enough to compact the soil around the plants and get rid of any air pockets, but with larger seedlings such as cucumbers and tomatoes, it is worth pressing around them a bit with your hands.

After planting

The best indication of successful planting is seeing new leaf growth within a few days after transplanting. This means that the transition from tray to garden went smoothly. If new leaf growth doesn't happen quickly, don't despair – it is a learning opportunity. The plant's health might not be optimal but it can still be a healthy and productive plant.

Sourcing seeds

Using good-quality seeds is fundamental to successful gardening. You can do the best job in every aspect, but if your seeds have not been well bred, your plants will be more prone to disease, or not produce a bountiful harvest.

Every time a grower saves seeds from a crop, they are effectively breeding seeds. Seed growers need to continually breed varieties to handle the current disease pressure, as well as being true to type and high-yielding. It takes a lot of attention to do this well, and seed companies are often financially pressed to take shortcuts.

We are huge advocates for using open-pollinated varieties as much as possible, and there are great seed-lines out there to choose from. Unfortunately, the billions of dollars invested in the seed industry are mostly for growing high-value hybrid varieties as that is where seed companies earn the most money.

Many heirloom varieties, which are open-pollinated but were named and recognised before World War II, are at times problematic because they are not always bred for modern disease resistance or high yields.

Using seeds that were grown organically should always be your

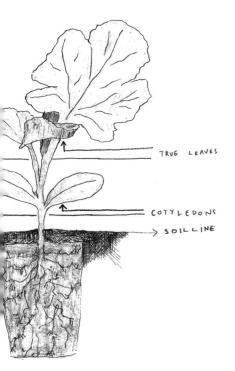

TRUE LEAVES

COTYLEDONS

→ SOIL LINE

Above Planting depth. On the left, lower than ground level. On the right, at ground level.

first choice. If there isn't a high-quality organic seed line available, consider using untreated conventional seeds. This means they most likely have been grown using chemicals, but that the seeds were not treated with fungicides after harvest.

Hybrid varieties can be organic. Hybrids are made by crossing two true-to-type open-pollinated seed lines. The first generation from this cross will produce extra vigorous offspring with certain predictable characteristics. However future generations will often have variable characteristics and will not perform reliably, making them problematic to save seeds from. In many of our trials, the majority of hybrid varieties outperformed open-pollinated varieties in yield when grown side by side, while also exhibiting excellent flavour. In some cases, using a hybrid variety was the single factor that doubled or even tripled our yield.

When choosing seeds, look for the following:

- Varieties that were bred for excellent flavour rather than good looks and uniformity.
- Varieties that were bred for high disease resistance.
- Varieties that were selected for early maturity, with the shortest date from sowing to harvest.
- Seeds that were grown under organic conditions as much as possible. If they are not available, only use untreated seeds, as fungicides will damage your soil biology.
- Choose the heaviest and largest seeds of the same variety. Larger seeds will almost always produce better plants.
- Always source the best seeds available, even if the price is higher. Good seeds save you money, space and time.
- When sowing seeds that are known to have a considerable variation between seedlings, sow 10–20 per cent more seedlings than you need to plant. This will allow you to plant only the best plants and then throw the rest away.

In the home garden, with its limited space, it is especially important to growing healthy, disease-resistant, high-yielding plants. Pay special attention to seed selection and do trials with different varieties of the same vegetable to find the ones that work best for you, in your garden.

Right Trellising and de-lateraling tomato plants in the tunnel house.

The Abundant Garden

Chapter 5
Productive planting

Allowing young plants to grow stress-free and undisturbed is crucial to their well-being and productivity. To do this, you will need to create conditions that allow continuous plant growth from seed to harvest.

Achieving continuous plant growth

There is a direct link between the stress that a plant experiences at different stages throughout its life and its overall yield. We illustrate this idea in the chart below (which is based on our personal observations, rather than hard data).

Here are the main situations that can cause stress in plants and interfere with continuous growth, and ways to avoid them:

Transplanting shock

Transplanting shock is what happens when a plant stops growing for two to three weeks after planting. This can happen for various reasons, such as:

- When a plant sits in its tray or pot for too long.
- When the transplant experiences rough handling.
- Inadequate watering during or after planting.
- When the conditions are very different between the propagation area and the garden, and the seedling didn't have a hardening-off period.

Plant growth in stress-free and stress-affected plants

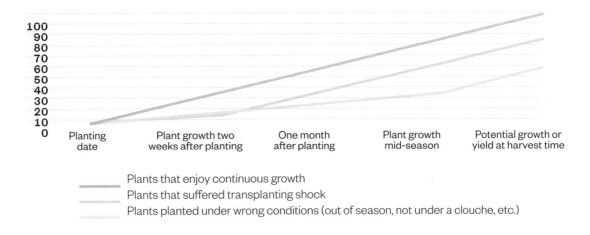

Planting date	Plant growth two weeks after planting	One month after planting	Plant growth mid-season	Potential growth or yield at harvest time

Plants that enjoy continuous growth
Plants that suffered transplanting shock
Plants planted under wrong conditions (out of season, not under a cloche, etc.)

Insufficient watering

Insufficient watering is a common problem when growing vegetables. Often when a crop is not doing well, adequately watering the growing area will solve the problem. Without sufficient moisture, soil organisms cannot function effectively and provide nutrients to your plants. We discuss irrigation in more detail in chapter 7.

Insufficient protection

A lack of protection from wind, sun and rain can cause a crop to become unnecessarily stressed. It's a common problem when growing a crop outside of its best planting window, but it can happen in any season.

One solution is to create a microclimate for your crops by growing them under cloches. By using the right cover for the plant, you can either heat or cool the crop and create a more stable environment.

In a tunnel house, temperatures can spike in a short time, and cause the plants to overheat. It is important to open up the tunnel house in the morning to encourage a gradual temperature change.

Severe weather events

Severe and uncharacteristic weather events are outside your control, and are becoming more frequent due to climate change. Extreme changes in temperature or light will negatively affect your plants. Summer crops that continuously suffer from temperature drops below their optimal range will never reach maximum productivity.

Protecting plants under cloches is not always enough to make plants thrive. The best strategy is to plant small amounts of the same crop at different times over the season (multiple successions), so that if an adverse weather event occurs and damages one succession, other successions of the same crop may be less affected. Even if all the successions in the field are compromised, your next succession won't be far away from being planted.

Pest pressure

Pests also put stress on crops, especially when the plants are growing outside their ideal climate conditions. The best way to deal with pest problems is to create a barrier between the pests and the crop, using a mesh cover that excludes them. Different meshes will be suitable for different pests. We discuss this further in chapter 10.

Insufficient soil fertility

Soil fertility is harder to remedy after the crop is planted; however, you still have some tools under your belt:

- Apply liquid fertiliser to the soil around your vegetable plants. This practice is referred to as a soil drench. It's highly effective, as it creates an immediate boost of nutrition available to your plants and food for the soil microbes. Dilute the concentrated fertilisers 1:10 to 1:20 with water in a watering can or bucket. Apply a few litres per square metre close to your plants after watering and repeat the application every week or two. If you don't have a liquid feed available, you can apply a powdered fertiliser, such as fish meal, and water it down.

- Apply a foliar spray to the leaves of the plants, covering as much surface area as possible. Plants quickly respond to this type of liquid feeding, and you can repeat this application every week or two, or even daily. Dilute with water at a 1:50 to 1:100 ratio.
- Apply an additional layer of compost over the soil's surface if the planting density allows it, and water well. It takes a week or two for plants to respond to this application, but the effect of the compost will be more substantial and longer lasting than liquid feeds.

Use all three application methods for the best chance of success. Once the crops are harvested, it is easier to make adjustments to the soil to improve future planting conditions.

By taking good care of your plants, paying attention to the conditions that help them thrive and reducing the possibility that they will become stunted, you will be able to grow healthier plants and have a more bountiful harvest.

Intensive cropping and high crop turnover

For the garden to fulfil its productive potential, it's important to keep it in constant production. Our general rule is that as soon as one crop comes out, another goes in. You don't have to wait for a whole bed to clear to plant a new crop; if you have harvested half of your carrots, you could plant something new in their place. As much as possible, try to harvest in blocks, clearing a whole area rather than spot harvesting throughout the bed, as it makes replanting easier.

With intensive cropping, you can grow multiple crops in the same bed throughout the season. We usually plant between three and eight crops per bed in a season. Some crops can stay in the bed for up to eight months (such as cucumbers and tomatoes), and some for as little as four weeks (such as rocket and radishes in the summer). All bed space is valuable when you realise how many plants can grow in just one square metre! (See table overleaf.) Cropping this way increases the organic matter in the soil from year to year, embedding

Above Lettuce planted in a diagonal spacing pattern.

organic matter into the soil from the plant roots you leave in the ground as about 50 per cent of a plant's mass is in its roots.

To make the best use of your garden space, try to replant or sow a bed within a few days of the most recent harvest. Plants help to grow plants. The more complex the biological interactions between plants and soil microbes, the better the conditions will be for future plants. Introducing new plants as closely as possible to the removal of older ones gives the new plants a growing boost. In some cases, you can interplant established plants with new ones, for seamless crop continuity.

Close spacing and high-density planting

To protect the soil and to avoid weeds popping up, you can create a living mulch by planting or sowing your bed as densely as possible. The planting density can vary; it depends at what stage you want to harvest your crops. The key is to plant densely without compromising yield and harvesting efficiencies. Sometimes less is more, so although we encourage you to experiment, start with using the recommendations on the seed packets.

Your goal should be to achieve full leaf cover as soon as possible, typically within three to six weeks from planting or sowing. You will know you've nailed it when plants touch each other without overlapping. This living mulch protects your soil from erosion, discourages weeds from germinating under the low light sub-canopy conditions, keeps the soil moist, reduces evaporation, and of course, more plants provide more produce for you.

It takes time to learn the vigour and size of each plant variety you are using, and at what stage you prefer to harvest your crop. With attention to detail over a couple of seasons, you can learn this for most vegetables. You can experiment when growing a new crop, or if you think there might be a better way of spacing than you are currently using. Divide the bed into two parts, one with your tried-and-true method and the other with the method you think might work better. When it's time to harvest, compare the two parts for yield, health and size to decide which one works best for you. Sometimes closer spacing means smaller-sized vegetables, and it is personal preference as to whether you want fewer, larger vegetables or many smaller ones. Sometimes the choice to plant

Below Kohlrabi and cape gooseberry interplanted to maximise bed space.

How many plants can fit in one square metre (10.7 sq ft) and their average yield

Vegetable	Potential Number of Plants per one square metre (10.7 sq ft)	Average Yield* per one square metre (10.7 sq ft)
Basil	20	8 kg (17.6 lb)
Bean	80 bush, 20 climbing	3.5 kg (7.7 lb)
Beetroot	60	12 kg+ (26.4 lb+)
Broad Bean	30	2 kg (4.4 lb)
Broccoli, Cabbage and Cauliflower	9	6.5, 20 and 14 kg (14.3, 44 and 30.8 lb)
Capsicum, Chilli Pepper	9	4 kg (8.8 lb)
Carrots	250	15 kg+ (33 lb+)
Celery	20	18 kg (39.6 lb)
Coriander, Dill	200	4 kg (8.8 lb)
Courgette (summer squash), Pumpkin	1	9 kg+ (19.8 lb+)
Cucumber	4	24 kg (52.8 lb)
Eggplant	9	6 kg (13.2 lb)
Fennel	20	8 kg (17.6 lb)
Garlic	30	2 kg (2.4 lb)
Kale	12	9 kg (19.8 lb)
Leek, Onion	36	8 kg (17.6 lb)
Lettuce, Endive, Kohlrabi	25	4 kg (8.8 lb)
Parsley	36	2.5 kg (5.5 lb)
Parsnip	100	15 kg (33.3 lb)
Pea	80 bush, 40 climbing	1.3 kg (2.86 lb)
Potato	6	10 kg+ (2.2 lb+)
Rock melon, Watermelon, Butternut (Winter squash)	10	12 kg+ (26.4+)
Radish and Turnip	200	6 kg (13.2 lb)
Rocket	200	1.5 kg (3.3 lb)
Spinach	100	13 kg (28.6)
Sweet corn	12	3.5 kg (7.7 lb)
Tomato	4	10 kg (22 lb)

* These numbers are estimated based on an average yield and can vary significantly depending on local conditions, soil fertility, variety, water input, plant vigour and how long the crop is in the ground.

Grid

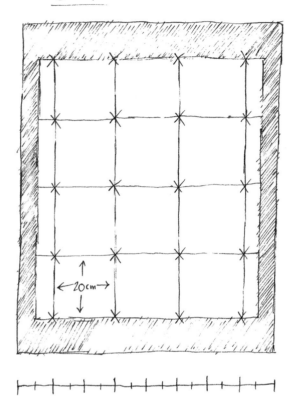

Diagonal

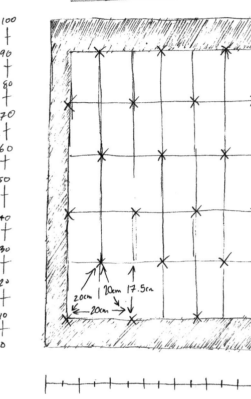

100
90
80
70
60
50
40
30
20
10
0

20cm

20cm | 20cm | 17.5cm
20cm

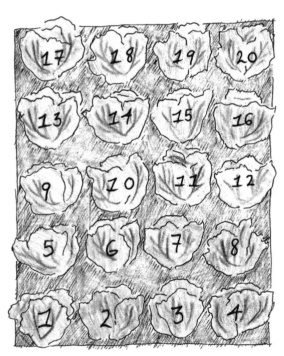

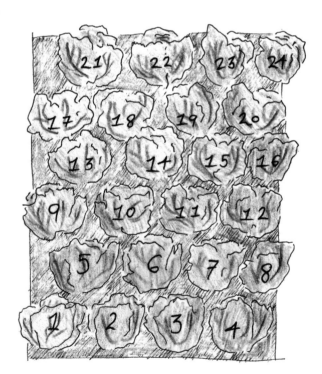

more densely will result in a lower yield per plant, but a higher yield per square metre.

One of the most common mistakes that beginner gardeners make is spacing plants too closely. It is best to first learn what each crop is supposed to look like when it is healthy and well spaced, before trying to create space-saving combinations.

A good way to increase planting density is to plant crops in a staggered pattern that is based on diagonal spacing. Diagonal spacing allows you to fill up the bed with 10–15 per cent more plants. Let's take kohlrabi as an example. Kohlrabi can be planted at 20 cm (8 inch) spacing. If we have an 80 cm (32 inch) wide bed, on a grid pattern based on squares, that means four plants in a row over five rows, totalling 20 plants. With diagonal spacing, there are still 4 plants in a row, but now the rows can be 3.5 cm closer, while still keeping the 20 cm (8 inch) spacing between each plant. This 'frees up' another 17.5 cm (7 inches), which is almost another row's worth. For every five regular grid-based rows, you could fit six diagonally spaced rows.

Companion planting and planting patterns

There are endless combinations and spacing variations when planting vegetables. Companion planting is the interplanting of two or more different crops, and it is quite an art to get it right! There are many myths surrounding companion planting, which often seem to be based on wishful thinking rather than researched techniques. We have had our fair share of both successes and failures, as we try to push the boundaries of what's possible. Cropping multiple vegetables from the same garden bed can work really well, but it does take practice to get it right.

Ideally, interplanted crops have beneficial symbiotic effects on each other, or at least one plant benefits from being planted alongside the other. A well-known combination is growing tomatoes, marigolds and basil together. The marigolds repel harmful soil nematodes, and the aromatic basil repels above-ground pests. The tomatoes grow up a pole or trellis, while the basil and marigold grow in a bushy shape underneath, acting as a

Left above Diagonal spacing allows you to plant more rows in the same length of garden bed compared with grid planting.

Left below Grid versus diagonal planting of lettuce.

The Abundant Garden

living mulch. The basil particularly enjoys a bit of extra shade from the tomatoes during the warm summer days.

Sometimes companion planting is designed for the plants to complement each other's growing space, both above and under the ground. The 'guild of the three sisters' is a successful traditional Native American trio, comprising corn, climbing beans and squash. This combination has a triple symbiotic effect: while the beans fix nitrogen for their own benefit, some of it becomes available for the corn and squash, and the corn is used as a growing structure for the beans. The beans also provide a living mulch while climbing on the corn and the squash. To do this successfully, sow or plant the corn first, followed by the beans and squash a few weeks later. The squash also needs to be a less vigorous variety, or you will struggle to get to the beans and corn. Although the overall yield of this combination will be higher than any plant planted alone, you will get less from each individual plant, as the plants will need to be spaced further apart than they usually would be when planted as a crop by themselves.

We generally only interplant if there is a definite advantage in doing so; if there isn't, we simply plant each vegetable in a separate cluster. Vegetables don't have to be intertwined to create a beautiful, diverse garden. In natural environments, it is common to see clusters of plants growing together.

We mostly use intercropping when there is an opportunity to grow a fast-growing crop in the gaps left between slower-growing vegetables. This allows us to double up on the bed space and achieve a temporary ground cover while the slower, longer-season crops are still being established. Other advantages include maximising the diversity of insects and beneficial organisms, and sharing resources such as row cover and irrigation.

Creating good planting combinations depends on many factors to work well, and what works for another gardener might not work for you. These factors include:

- The time of year. What works in one season won't work in another.
- Soil condition and bed tilth. Crops that are planted far apart such as pumpkins won't need as fine tilth as a sowed crop.

Left Intensive cropping.

Above Companion planting garlic, rocket and radish.

The Abundant Garden

- Watering. The crops should enjoy the same style of watering.
- Pest pressure. The crops have similar crop-protection needs.
- Plant growing speed and size at maturity. The plants grow proportionate to each other, so one doesn't smother the other.

Here's an example of the effect of the time of the year on interplanting. When courgettes or cucumbers are planted in the early spring, they grow slowly and take about 8–10 weeks to fill up the bed. In that time, you can safely grow one or two rows of a quick crop on the perimeter of the bed, and even a few plants in between them. We usually plant beets, lettuce, kohlrabi, and sow salad turnips or radishes. If the courgettes and cucumber are planted in early summer, it only takes them about four weeks to fill up the bed, so it's no longer suitable to interplant with the other plants except for radishes. Still, they will only grow well if the bed gets frequent watering, which you might not want to do, as the courgettes only need to be watered around the base of their stem in the first few weeks, and you will have fewer weeds germinating if you only water the courgettes. In the spring, the plants don't tend to need much additional watering as naturally occurring rain will usually be enough.

Some planting combinations are supposed to be detrimental to each other. For example, coniferous trees secrete allelopathic substances that discourage other plants from germinating. We have been warned that the strongly aromatic herb fennel negatively affects plant growth in its neighbours; although we generally plant fennel in a cluster rather than interplanting with other varieties, we have never noticed nearby plants being affected.

Another variation of companion planting is relay planting, in which a second crop is planted into a bed of an already established crop. Relay planting might be a good idea if it isn't convenient to plant both crops at the same time, or if a plant is on the way out, and you can plant a new crop that uses the protection of the old crop to get established. The new plants can also enjoy ongoing microbial activity from the original crop.

When planting tomatoes, you can plant them in a bed of a growing crop such as beets. Once the beets are removed, spread a layer of compost on the bed to feed the tomatoes and follow up by interplanting basil and marigolds.

An opportunity to interplant also arises when a crop has only partially germinated, or if a pest damages a large portion but you don't want to remove it completely. Fill in the gaps with another crop that can be harvested within a similar timeframe. For example, patchy carrot beds can be interplanted with beets. You need to act quickly however, as you don't want the beets to need another month to grow when the carrots are ready to come out! Although you can relay plant constantly, it is handy to have a bed completely empty at some point so it can be used for a crop that takes a lot of space and needs to go into the ground all at once, such as kūmara (sweet potato).

Perennial herbs, which can live in the garden for many years, and seasonal annual flowers make a lovely addition to a garden. Herbs and flowers attract beneficial insects and repel certain pests. Sometimes they attract pests that are already present in the garden, which can help bring them to your attention before they overtake your vegetables (like a canary in the mine) or even act as a decoy that you can throw to the chickens, who will enjoy the extra protein.

Whether you cut flowers to put in a vase or eat the edible varieties, flowers in or around the garden are well worth having. You can place them at the edge of beds, in the centre of a wide bed or in a bed of their own. A friendly warning: herbs like to expand and flowers tend to drop seeds and germinate for years to come. This can be a good thing, but don't hesitate to cut plants back or remove seedlings if they appear where you don't want them.

Constructing a companion-planting combination is like designing a three-dimensional model that changes over time. In practice, you will usually do well if you space the two crops by considering their full size at maturity and dividing it by two. Another approach is to calculate when the main crop will use all the bed space, then figure out how many weeks are available for companion planting, and research what plant varieties can mature in this timeframe.

We encourage you to learn each variety's growing habits on its own prior to interplanting with other crops. There are significant variations in varieties within the same vegetable group, and vegetables grow at different rates throughout the year, so don't be discouraged if the match isn't perfect. Be adaptable and prepare to sacrifice one of your crops or harvest it early if necessary, so as not to compromise your main crop.

Right above Companion planting of transplanted courgette with direct-seeded radish.

Right below Calendula (pot marigold).

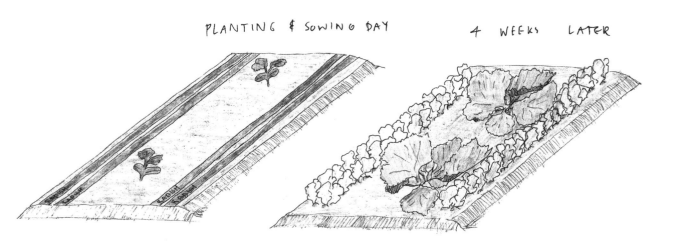

PLANTING & SOWING DAY   4 WEEKS LATER

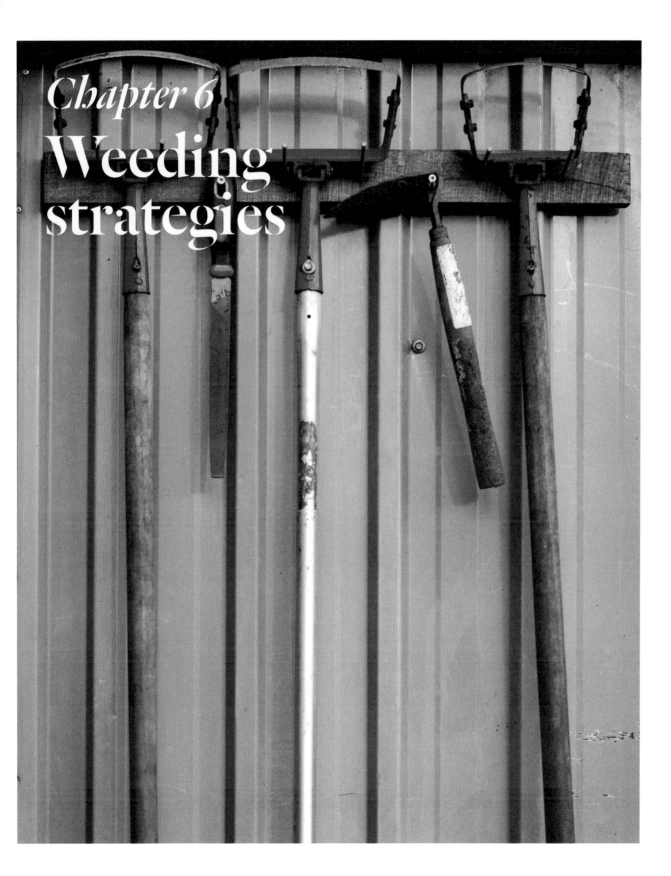

Chapter 6
Weeding strategies

One of the best ways to maintain a productive garden without hours and hours of labour is to keep the garden as weed-free as possible.

Keeping your garden weedfree

After eliminating any existing established weeds (by using tarps, heavy mulch or any of the other methods described earlier in this book), going forward you'll only need to deal with weeds that germinate from seeds. Easy!

Page 113 Two large hoes, a file, niwashi and a medium stirrup hoe.

The Abundant Garden

There are three main strategies we use to establish a weed-free garden. The first is getting rid of the pre-existing weed seeds in the soil, known as the 'soil's seed bank', through short, regular weeding sessions. Seeds can remain dormant until favourable conditions prompt them to grow, so it will take a few seasons to completely exhaust the seed bank, and the wind will continue to blow new seeds onto the beds as well. The trick is to weed little and often; removing weeds when they are small is much easier than when they are established.

The second strategy for a weed-free garden is to avoid soil disturbance using no-till practices. By keeping the soil layers intact, seeds located deep in the soil are not brought to the surface, where the light and warmth will encourage them to germinate.

The final strategy is not to let any weeds get established in the garden. Once weeds are established, they can quickly take over big portions of your cultivated beds, making them even harder to remove. Established weeds develop large quantities of viable seeds, which, once dispersed throughout the garden, will undermine your previous weeding efforts. As the saying goes, 'one year's seeds makes seven years of weeds'.

In general, if you think you can see seeds on the plant, those seeds will be viable. Remove these plants carefully, so they don't drop seeds into the growing bed. These plants should not go directly onto the compost heap. Instead, they can be fed to the chickens or soaked in a bucket of water for a week before being added to the compost pile.

Weeds will always pop up in your garden, but as you work to decrease their number, your workload will also significantly decrease in the years to come.

Weeding tools

We do most of our weeding with two styles of hoe: one has a long handle about our height, and the other has a short handle about 25 cm long (10 inches). With this combination of quality hoes, we're able to reach any weeds that dare to show themselves.

Keep the blades of the hoe sharp by giving them a quick sharpen with a file before you start weeding. Just like a chef wouldn't work with a blunt knife, a gardener shouldn't use a blunt hoe. A sharp hoe will effortlessly cut weeds, rather than just bruising them and moving them around the bed. This makes weeding physically easier and also more effective, as most young weeds won't recover from their roots being separated from the stem.

There are many types of hoes of different shapes and sizes. We love our long-handled stirrup hoes (also called oscillating hoes) for most weeding tasks and find that the 12.5 cm (5 inch) width is the most useful size. The Japanese or Korean niwashi is our favourite short-handled weeding tool, and is basically a sharp blade on a stick. The niwashi is a versatile tool that can also be used as a trowel.

Weeding basics

When weeding, timing is everything. It's important to do your weeding when the ground is as dry as possible (without damaging crops of course). When the soil is moist from rain or watering, weeds re-root themselves more easily. Aim to weed on a sunny morning, when the sun is beating down, as even large weeds will dry out. Usually, after a few sunny hours, you can turn the irrigation back on. In winter, you will need to pick up most of the weeds you have cut, because they are likely to re-establish themselves if you leave them on the soil.

If there are a lot of weeds in the area where you are planning your garden, you could space your rows so their width matches one of your hoes for efficient weeding. We've found this approach hugely helpful when we are establishing a new garden bed.

Weeding doesn't have to happen only in predetermined weeding sessions. When you are harvesting vegetables and encounter a patch with weeds, it's worth spending a few minutes to pull them out. If you are already bending down to harvest, take the opportunity to pull out a few weeds as well. Developing a mentality of 'let's take care of it', rather than 'leave it for later' goes a long way towards creating a productive garden.

Although weeds will come up throughout the year, you will have spikes of weed pressure at certain times depending on which

Right Yotam sharpening the stirrup hoe.

weeds are predominant in your area. Spring is usually one of these times, as weeds try to grow before the dry weather kicks in. In our garden, there is also a spike in autumn, and we make sure to concentrate our weeding around that time, so we can start the winter with no established weeds.

Repeated shallow cultivation

Weeding with a hoe is more effective when you hit weeds while they are tiny. Once weeds grow larger than about 5 cm (2 inches) tall, they don't die as easily, and it takes significantly more time and effort to weed them. Aim to cut the plants with the hoe, just below the ground so that the leaves are separated from the roots. When plants are young, they rarely recover from this trauma.

In addition to cutting them, young, small weeds can be smothered with a thin layer of soil. Both these strategies allow the weeds to be eliminated without causing a significant disturbance to the soil, as well as leaving the roots' biomass to decompose in the ground and feed the soil's biological community. Generally, it's best to avoid pulling weeds, as it takes organic matter from the soil and causes a disturbance that will often give birth to a new flush of weeds.

When weed pressure is high, hoe the paths and beds every two or three weeks to tackle the weeds when they are vulnerable. This will make a big impact and make weeding easier in future years. It usually takes up to two hours to skim through our 1000 square metre (10,764 square feet) garden.

When working with a long-handled hoe, hold the hoe with your thumbs facing up. This helps to keep your back straight and your shoulders broad, maintaining good body posture while doing most of the weeding while standing up. Try it; you'll be amazed to feel the difference between thumbs up and thumbs down, and how your muscles respond to each position. If you get tired or if the weeds are 5–15 cm (2–6 inches) tall, switch to thumbs down so you can apply more force. For weeds larger than 15 cm (6 inches), it is usually better to skim them off at ground level with a spade.

Right Niva harvesting edible alyssum flowers.

The Abundant Garden

The stale-bed technique

One of the best weeding practices is to weed before your crops are even in the ground. Do this by tricking the weeds into growing; by preparing the bed and keeping it moist, but not planting anything into it, you will create favourable conditions for weeds to germinate. After 10 days to two weeks, a flush of weeds will pop up; hoe the bed to kill these weeds then keep it dry for another day. Once the weed pressure had reduced, it's time to plant or sow the vegetables you want to grow.

Covering beds

When a bed is not in use or not going to be planted or sown in a couple of weeks, it is best to cover it with weedmat, tarps or heavy mulch. This helps to protect the soil biology, prevents soil erosion and compaction by rain, and stops the bed from growing a crop of weeds.

Weeds aren't evil

We do also want to say that weeds are not evil! Most plants we consider weeds are usually the first to colonise bare land after a natural disaster. They have an important ecological function as pioneer plants that protect the soil. While they are growing, they improve the conditions for other long-term plants to flourish, and in the meantime, they also feed the soil's biology.

Many weeds also have medicinal properties, some are edible, and many will flower and provide food for bees and beneficial insects. However, you really don't want them in your vegetable gardens, so you should systematically get rid of them . . . but there is no need to resent them while you're doing so.

Chapter 7
Irrigation and watering

Water is essential for all living organisms, and plants and soil biology are no exception. When correctly watered, the microorganisms in your soil can perform their essential functions, and in turn, this enhanced soil-biology activity will feed your plants.

How much water?

Having the correct moisture level in your soil is one of the most critical factors in successful vegetable growing.

Growing vegetables require moisture levels ranging from 40–70 per cent. You can get an indication of your soil moisture levels by taking a handful of soil and squeezing it tightly:

The Abundant Garden

- If it's dripping water, the moisture content will be around 80 per cent. Be careful not to overwater, as conditions can become anaerobic.
- If no water comes out, but your hand is stained from the soil, the moisture content is in the ideal 40–70 per cent range.
- If no water comes out, and your hand is not stained, the moisture content is less than 40 per cent. It's time to water.

If a crop isn't thriving, the first thing to check is that the soil is moist. We find that inaccurate watering is the cause of almost all problems in our garden; fortunately, the solution is simply to adjust watering levels to achieve appropriate soil moisture. In a garden's natural environment, with plants at different sizes and stages, all with different watering needs and ground cover, it is a challenge to get watering right in all the beds all of the time. Luckily, there is a wide range of acceptable soil-moisture levels, and it is not the end of the world to skew this dynamic balance for short periods. Of course, you should aim to avoid extremes; very dry conditions will stress your plants, and oversaturation will cause anaerobic conditions. Both extremes weaken the plants and make them more susceptible to pests and disease.

Below Watermelon planted with drip irrigation.

Checking soil-moisture levels

Check the soil's moisture at a depth of about 20 cm (8 inches). It's a classic mistake to think the soil has been adequately watered when in fact only the top few centimetres of the soil are wet. If you have had a long break since the last watering and the ground has dried out, you will need to be very thorough in your next watering to carry moisture all the way down. One short watering session is unlikely to penetrate through all the soil's layers.

It is tricky to get water into clay and silt-dominated soils, which tend to repel water when they are dry. It usually requires double or even triple the amount of water you would need for a regular watering session. You could do two or three consecutive waterings or a gentle spray over a longer time. You will sometimes notice that in the summer when it rains, farmers will turn on their irrigation! Rain helps the soil to accept water.

The amount of time it takes to bring the moisture levels to

desired levels fluctuates between soils, climate, crops and time of year, so your best bet is to get in there and check the moisture levels often, in different locations throughout the garden.

After some time, you will develop a gardener's intuition and will not need to test the soil as frequently. You will also *learn to read your plants and water them before they start to wilt.* Plants generally buzz with health after a good rain, and they respond similarly when the moisture is adequate. It depends on the vegetable, but many types of plants will become erect when well-watered. However some plants, such as members of the Cucurbit family (courgettes, pumpkin, cucumber) tend to deliberately wilt their leaves to minimise evaporation during the hot hours of the day and no amount of water will change that!

Water the soil, not the plants

By watering your garden thoroughly, and not just the little area next to each plant, you are encouraging your plants to extend their roots to a larger area. This makes plants more robust and allows them to access more nutrients.

Most roots and biological activity are concentrated in the top 5–10 cm (2–4 inches) of the soil. Although plants will grow even if this layer dries out, they will thrive if this layer is kept moist.

When plants are getting established, you will need to water them frequently so the soil stays continuously moist. Frequent watering is important for both direct-seeded plants at the germination stage and newly planted transplants. If the soil around the plants dries out at this delicate establishment stage, the plants will be permanently stressed and may even die.

When you have wide spacing between your plants, such as with squashes, and your water supply is limited, you can water safely just around the plants for a week or so and increase that diameter every week. Even so, we water the whole bed if possible, to support the soil microorganisms, and encourage weed germination, which we can hoe while the other plants are still young and there is easy access.

Pay special attention to watering around your garden's edges. The edges of your garden beds are more prone to drying out from

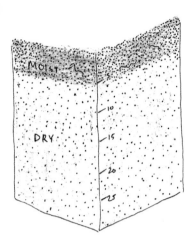
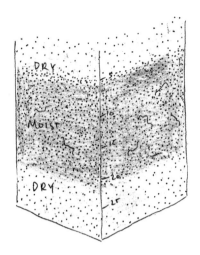
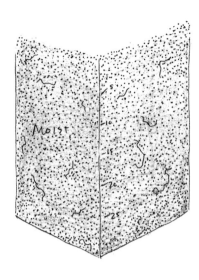

Above Watering the soil — on the left, only the top 5 cm are moist. In the middle, there is a hidden dry layer below the moist layer. On the right, this is the ideal soil moisture.

the wind and sun, and this often means you will need to water the perimeter of the garden more than the middle of the bed. Watering the edges helps to prevent your soil from drying out, and you will enjoy better growth around these growing areas.

Sometimes it's helpful to water the path beside your garden as well. If you stop watering just at the edge of your growing area, but the soil is bone dry beyond it, your bed will dry out faster due to the capillary action that will draw the water out of your beds. Over summer, lay a thick layer of mulch to help keep the ground, the edges and paths around the garden edges moist. Over winter in wet, temperate climates, it is often best to rake the mulch and compost it, as it tends to be a breeding ground for slugs and snails.

Time of day to water

If your plants are wilting, you are better to water right then, and not wait for the perfect time of day to water. If you have only a specific window of time during the day when you are able to water your garden, that will also be just fine. Don't stress about the time of day if you can't control it.

But, if you have the choice, some parts of the day are better for watering than others, especially if you're watering with sprinklers or a hose. Our preferred watering time is in the late afternoon, two to three hours before the sun sets. This allows plants to dry out before nightfall, while the soil stays nicely moist until around noon the next day. *It is better for plants not to go into the night wet;* wet foliage is an invitation for fungal diseases which weaken the plants.

Mornings are another good time to water your garden. For best results and better plant growth, wait until the sun has come up over the horizon. While the morning sun will dry the plants' foliage from excess moisture, it will also raise the ground's temperature so that plant growth is not affected from the cold water. The humidity that naturally occurs during summer nights condenses on plants as dew and can encourage fungal diseases. It is best to water while the dew is still on the plants, to avoid extending the amount of time that plants are wet.

Avoid watering in the middle of sunny summer days, as much of the water will be lost to evaporation.

Choosing a watering technique

When deciding the best way to water each crop, think about the plant's natural watering patterns according to its evolutionary context. The vegetables you grow originated in different parts of the world. Matching your watering method to the climate and the time of year in which the plants naturally grow will result in substantially healthier and higher-yielding plants.

Below Watering viola.

There are three categories of plants to consider when watering:

1. Plants that prefer watering from above can be watered with a sprinkler or a hose spray. These are plants originally from areas with frequent summer rains, wet springs, or close to streams, and include most leafy greens.
2. Plants that prefer not to be watered from above can be watered with a drip line, or by watering the ground and avoiding wetting the leaves. These are plants that evolved to grow during hot, dry summers, and include tomatoes, cucumber, courgettes, squash and pumpkins.
3. Plants that can be watered by either method. This group is mostly root vegetables, but most greens will also grow well as long as they are well watered.

Smart water use

As weather patterns change throughout the globe due to climate disruption, summer droughts have become a serious issue in Aotearoa New Zealand, as well as in other parts of the world. Gardeners and farmers alike must be mindful of making the best use of available water and conserving it whenever possible.

Here are some water-saving strategies for the home gardener.

- *Shelter your gardens from the wind,* using shelter belts of perennial native vegetation or windbreak cloth. This will dramatically reduce evaporation of soil moisture and reduce your need to irrigate.
- *Place your beds on the contour of the land*, perpendicular to the slope, which will help slow down the run-off of water away from the garden and maximise absorption both during rain events and while watering.
- *Increase the organic matter component in your soil,* as it can store several times its weight in water. This is another advantage of the no-till method. As you minimise soil disturbance, incorporate organic matter (compost, mulch, biochar), grow healthy plants and keep their roots in the soil, and grow cover crops, you will be able to hold more water in the soil.
- *Use mulch to prevent soil from drying out.* Mulching is a really good way to keep moisture levels constant. You can either use landscape fabrics or organic mulches such as woodchips. Organic mulches help to improve soil quality over time. Lay mulch on the paths and around your plants. Remember that mulches containing carbon take nitrogen from the soil and are best aged before being applied. Waiting a few weeks before planting into them or supplementing with a nitrogen-rich foliar feed will do the trick.
- *If your soil drains quickly, minimise the amount of forking and bed aeration during the spring and summer.* Forking improves the soil's ability to drain and can be counterproductive in certain soils when water is limited. Although plants prefer a relatively loose soil to grow their roots, adequate soil-moisture levels play an even more

important role in keeping plants happy and healthy.

- *Choose drip irrigation as your primary watering technique.*
- *Adopt a watering regime that encourages deep roots.* Once transplants have acclimated to the new bed or seedlings have germinated, you can gradually increase the time between watering. The idea is to encourage the plants to send their roots deeper into the soil, to access water from the new depth. Over a period of several weeks, you can move from watering every day to watering every three to four days. Pay attention that the plants don't wilt or become stressed, as this can lead to early bolting (producing premature seeds instead of growing) and other problems.
- *Establish your main crops of tomatoes, potatoes, cucumbers, courgettes, eggplant and so on in the spring,* when there is naturally ample soil moisture. As summer approaches, your plants will be well established and will need less frequent watering, compared to planting them in the summer.
- *Grow summer crops that require less water,* as opposed to growing young delicate greens. Many vegetable varieties have been bred to need less water, although unfortunately they are not always commonly available to buy. Crops that generally need less water include tomatoes, eggplants, cucumbers, squash, melons, beans, potatoes and kūmara (sweet potato).
- *Keep your garden weed-free.* As vegetable plants grow, they use water for transpiration. Depending on the plant type, it can take a plant a hundred times its weight in water to grow the equivalent biomass. For example, it can take 770 litres (1600 pints) of water for a corn plant to grow 1 kg (2.2 pounds) of plant biomass. By keeping your garden weed-free, you are not wasting water on growing weeds.
- *Water in the late afternoons.*
- In the summer, *plant in the evening or on rainy days.*
- If you are short of water but not on space, *increase the spacing between plants.* This will reduce the competition for water between plants and allows individual plants to access more water. Close spacing of plants creates a living mulch, but also increases the garden's water needs significantly. Spacing plants further apart encourages plants to become

stocky and invest in root growth, whereas plants that are close together tend to focus on growing taller to reach sunlight and have higher water needs.

- *Plant deeper.* When planting, make dimples in the soil around your plants, creating small funnels to accumulate more water. The plants will get more water because they are planted more deeply. This works better for larger seedlings. When direct seeding in the bed, create a deep furrow into which you can sow your seeds.
- *Avoid installing raised beds.*
- *Consider using wicking-bed containers* and mulching them. Wicking beds are built by dividing any size container horizontally in two and can even be installed on large timber-frame raised beds, using a drinking-water-grade liner. The bottom third of the container is the water

Below Wicking bed.

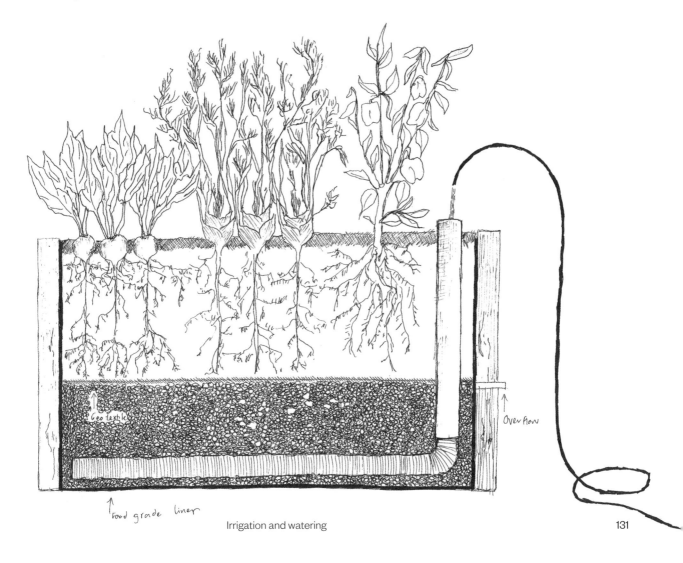

Geo textile

Over flow

Food grade liner

reservoir, the top two-thirds layer is the growing media, and a permeable geotextile (such as weedmat) fabric sits in between to keep the two layers apart. The growing media stays moist through capillary action, which moves the water from the lower level as needed.

- While plants get established, they need watering from above, but afterwards, you will only need to fill the water reservoir to keep the plants well-watered. As water can't escape from the bottom, any water entering this system will be used by your plants. As there is no surface water, this method also tends to have fewer weeds, because they can't germinate.

- The bottom layer should be filled with small stones, around 5–7 mm (0.2–0.3 inches) diameter, spread around a perforated pipe. The perforated pipe should also act as an access pipe (see illustration on page 131) to add water into the system. Install an overflow pipe at the height of the geotextile, to indicate when the reservoir is full, and a tap at the bottom for drainage. Before filling the container, make sure it doesn't leak.

Water resilience

As well as minimising the amount of water your garden needs, you might want to consider installing extra water reservoirs for dry summers. As droughts intensify, towns and cities around the world are asking residents not to water their gardens in the summer. *Installing rainwater collection systems or even a tank that can be filled with town-supply water in winter can make a huge difference to your ability to guarantee water for your gardens in summer.*

Although the amount of water you need changes a lot between soils and locations, *1 square metre (10.7 square feet) of garden requires approximately 3.5–7 litres a day during a hot summer.* In a dry summer, garden of 10 square meters (107 square feet) would require 4400–8800 litres of water during a four-month period. These numbers may seem high, but they are probably even higher for commercial growers. Plants need water to grow, and vegetables are well worth the investment.

Don't be discouraged if you have a limited amount of water

Below Hand watering.

The Abundant Garden

available, as many crops can cope with lower amounts of water and still provide ample yields.

If you want a large garden but lack the means to water it in summer, then plan for a fantastic winter garden. In most temperate climates, there is almost no need to do any watering during winter. Start planting and sowing with the autumn rains and continue planting all the way into spring. In summer, plan for a smaller garden with fewer crops, and focus on growing plants with low watering requirements and cover crops.

Watering systems

There are three main techniques for watering the garden: hand watering, drip irrigation and sprinklers. Each of these methods has advantages and disadvantages. You might choose a combination of them for your garden, depending on water access, personal preference and climate.

Hand watering

Hands down, hand watering is the most accurate and engaging watering technique. When you hand water, you spend more time with your plants. You get to observe and connect with them, which allows you to better gauge plant health and notice anything that needs to be done, such as weeding, resolving poor germination, fertiliser boosting, trellising or harvesting. It is an enjoyable and relaxing task, it will make you a better gardener and you will have better yields this way. With hand watering, you can be relatively accurate, delivering the water where you want it to go. This is a significant advantage, as you can accommodate different beds and plants with the amount of water they need, depending on their size and watering needs.

To hand water efficiently, you will need relatively high-pressure water supply with a high flow rate, similar to what you expect inside your home. You can use a thumb to direct the water, or a high-quality nozzle with a gentle spray and full flow. When you are watering, it is best to direct the water upwards, creating an arc that softens the water impact. Avoid pointing the hose

directly at the ground, as the force of the water compacts the soil and splashes soil particles on to the plants, making them more susceptible to disease.

When purchasing a hose, we suggest a low-kink hose that doesn't leach any phthalates or heavy metals. If you are watering an extensive garden, consider using a 20 mm hose rather than the standard 13 mm, as it will allow much more water flow.

The downside of hand watering is that it is time-consuming. It can also take a bit of time to learn how to water plants effectively, as it is easy to underestimate how much water the soil needs to stay moist.

Designate a place to store your hose, and try to avoid leaving it on the ground as it will become a trip hazard. You could use an automatic retractable hose or hang the hose on a nearby wall or post.

Above Hand watering in an arc to soften the impact of the water on plants and soil.

Right Drip irrigation in action.

The Abundant Garden

Drip irrigation

Installing drip lines is more time-consuming and expensive than installing a sprinkler system that covers the same area, but has some crucial advantages:

- The water is distributed more accurately, and therefore saves water.
- Solanaceae, Cucurbits and many flowers grow better with drip irrigation.
- You can water any time of day, as the foliage doesn't get wet.
- Drip lines can be buried under weedmat or organic mulch, minimising evaporation.

There are a few types of drip-line systems, but we highly recommend a heavy-duty UV stabilised hose with built-in, pressure-compensating emitters at predetermined spacings. These pipes can last for decades if treated with care and can stay permanently on your garden beds. They also tend not to get blocked, compared to externally installed drippers.

Emitters are graded by litres per hour from each hole. For soils that are free draining, it is best to use low-flow emitters, as the gravity pull on the water is greater than the capillary action. With a low flow, around 1–1.6 litres/hour, the water will have time to spread rather than drop straight down.

When you install drip irrigation, test the watering area around the emitters below the ground, and use that information to decide how many lines you will need for a full bed cover. For our 80 cm (32 inch) wide beds, we use three lines 30 cm (12 inches) apart, with 30 cm (12 inches) between emitters. Although large rooting crops such as courgettes and tomatoes can grow with fewer lines, it is better to let the whole bed get fully moist so the plants have better nutrition.

When installing a drip-irrigation system, you will use tee, elbow and straight connectors, and ground staples to keep the lines in place. You can also install a small tap so that each bed can be turned off. It is crucial to attach a ratchet clip at every connection point to avoid the pipe disconnecting from the joiner.

The Abundant Garden

Installing a drip-irrigation system involves a lot of cutting, so consider investing in a tubing cutter to avoid injuries. If you use a knife, be sure to always cut against a piece of wood and not in the air to minimise the risk of injury.

Because the diameter of the drip lines is relatively small, 13 mm (0.5 inches), the water flow is restricted and the pressure will be dramatically reduced over long distances. This is nothing to worry about in a small garden, but once the garden is more substantial, you will need to use a larger diameter pipe, e.g. 25 mm (1 inch). Use a larger diameter pipe to bring the water to the beds, and then run the smaller diameter drip lines from that pipe onto the bed.

You can leave the drip line on the beds over winter, and flush them with clean water in spring. To flush the line, open the end of the irrigation line for a minute and run water through to let any dirt and insects out before you set them up for the season.

Sprinklers

Sprinklers are an effective way to spread water across a large area. There are many types of sprinklers; we recommend micro-sprinklers as they offer the best 'rain-like' spread and uniformity. Sprinklers can be permanently installed on stakes and posts, or they can be relocatable, such as oscillating sprinklers.

The main concern with all sprinklers is obtaining an even spread of water, so there aren't areas that get more water than others. Overwatering will cause plants to rot, and become diseased, while dry patches won't grow well. It's best to have a chat about your specific garden needs with the store you are purchasing the sprinklers from, as there are hundreds of variations to choose from.

Getting to know your water supply

When laying your irrigation, think about pressure, flow, access and filtration. If you are connected to mains water, you should have good pressure, flow and clean water. However, regardless of your water source, it is a good idea to install a mesh filter before running your sprinklers or drip irrigation to prevent particles blocking the irrigation. If you have your own water supply, you will need to make sure it has enough pressure and flow for efficient watering.

Regardless of how you water your plants, it's good to know how to measure your water supply (flow) output. This information helps you to determine how much time to spend watering, and which sprinklers to install. Take a bucket and measure how much time it takes to fill it when the tap is fully open. Your flow rate will be 60 divided by the amount of time (seconds) it took to fill up the bucket multiplied by the volume (litres) of the bucket [60 / measured seconds x litres = flow rate]. For example, a 10-litre bucket that takes 20 seconds to fill will have a flow rate of 60 / 20 x 10 = 30 litres per minute.

Let's say you want to water a 40 sqm vegetable garden, applying 5 litres of water per 1 sqm, with a flow rate of 30 litres per minute. To figure out how much time you would approximately need to spend watering, first let's figure out how many square metres you can water in a minute: 30 litres per minute divided by 5 litres per 1 sqm equals 6 sqm a minute. To water a 40 sqm garden, you would need just under 7 minutes (size divided by area watered per minute).

It's probably only worth checking your water pressure if you will be installing a comprehensive sprinkler system. To do this, you would need to attach a water-pressure metre, found at irrigation suppliers, to the end of your hose or irrigation pipe.

Making water accessible

A vegetable garden needs regular watering during weeks without rain; otherwise, the plants will stress and stop growing. Just one significant stress event can cause crop failure past the point of no return. To avoid skipping a watering session, you should make it as easy as possible to be able to water the garden. If the hose isn't within reach, it's too easy to skip an occasional watering. If you are using driplines or sprinklers, connect them directly to your main tap or hose, so they can easily be switched on.

Laying out and burying irrigation lines

When laying out your irrigation lines, you can either bury them or leave them above ground. If you are sure that you have the right pipes and location for your line, we suggest burying them as soon

Above Micro-sprinkler on a riser.

Right Manual timer.

as possible. (If you want to test it out first, that's fine.) A lot of pressure builds up in pipes when they heat up, and spraying your seedlings with hot water isn't a great idea!

When burying pipes, bury them 20 cm (8 inches) deep or more. Deeply buried pipes will be cooler, and there is less chance that someone will accidentally stick a fork in them. Lay your irrigation lines in easily locatable places in case you need to repair them. The centre of your paths or along fence lines is a good choice.

Irrigation timers and controllers

When using driplines or sprinklers, you can install a timer on your garden tap, to set the duration of the watering session so that it will be automatically turned off. A step further towards automation is to install an irrigation controller, which can fully automate your irrigation. An irrigation controller will help you keep the garden adequately watered and reduce the stress of daily watering by allowing you to schedule automatic watering sessions. You can also control the frequency and duration of each watering. The irrigation controller can be set to control more than one watering line, via an irrigation solenoid valve. This can be handy if one part of the garden is on drip irrigation, while another uses sprinklers.

When it comes to irrigation controllers, there are lots of gadgets you can enjoy. From rain sensors and soil-humidity sensors to mobile apps for remote control, you can keep the garden watered even when you are away.

Although we appreciate the convenience of our irrigation controller running our watering through dripline and sprinklers, and our set-up is relatively accurate, hand watering always gives better results. To make the automated irrigation system work well, you should monitor the soil moisture regularly and make frequent adjustments, including supplementing with hand watering as needed.

Fertigation

Fertigation is the term used to describe applying fertiliser through an irrigation system. You can use your water lines to add organic fertilisers and microbial inoculants to your crop, with a venturi fertiliser injector kit. The fertiliser can then be applied through hand watering with a hose, dripline or sprinklers. Fertigation is just another way of feeding your plants and soil microbes, to help your crops grow better, and is similar to applying fertilisers with a backpack sprayer. It works by filling a bucket with fertiliser, which the injector sucks up and feeds into the irrigation line. It is relatively cheap and straightforward to set up, but we found that using a smaller size injector works better than the larger ones when watering a small area. When installing a fertigation unit, be sure to install a non-return valve, so that fertiliser cannot enter and contaminate your main water supply.

Maintenance

If you are using a filter in your irrigation system, you will need to clean it periodically depending on how clean your water supply is. Otherwise, your flow will be reduced.

If the ground freezes in winter where you live, make sure to drain your drip and sprinkler lines before the temperatures drop. Water expands when it freezes, and can cause damage to irrigation lines. In spring, when it's time to turn the irrigation back on, check that water is spraying from every drip and sprinkler outlet, and clean any blockages you find.

Irrigation and watering

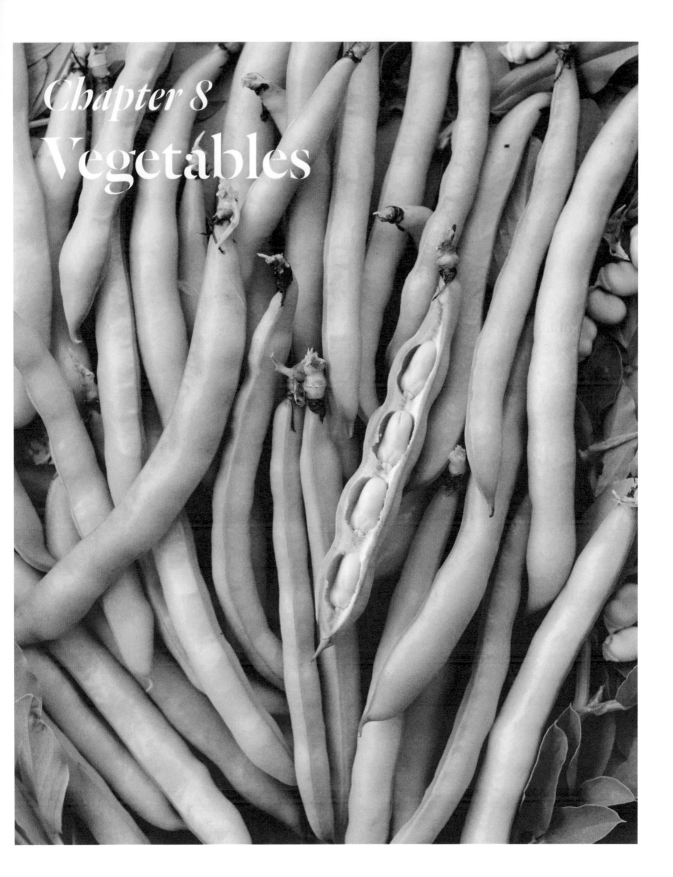

Chapter 8
Vegetables

In this chapter we've summarised a wealth of information about how to grow our favourite home-garden vegetables as well as various tips we've gleaned over the years.

Read this chapter alongside the other information we cover in this book. For example, many of the propagation techniques in this chapter build on the basic information set out in chapter 4. You'll then be able to use the information you learn in this chapter to create a crop plan for your garden, which we discuss in chapter 9.

Remember, all plants benefit from regular feeding and extra protection, which also allow you to extend your growing season. Different varieties of the same vegetable have size and flavour differences, and will often perform better in different seasons and environments. It is well worth trying a range of varieties and growing them side by side, to discover which ones you absolutely love and thrive in your garden. Look for varieties that are full of flavour, have vigorous growth, mature quickly, and are high-yielding and disease-resistant. Follow your tummy and always go for varieties with the best taste! Choose high-quality organic seeds if they are available.

Recommending vegetable varieties is tricky, as many seed lines come and go; however, if there is a well-preserved seed line we love, we'll mention it here.

Artichoke

Unlike most vegetables from the Asteraceae family, globe artichokes are perennial and can live for three to seven years in your garden. The harvest takes place over two months during late spring when there aren't many other vegetables around, making the delicious artichokes a real treat. The immature flower bud is the edible part of the artichoke plant. We steam them until the petals easily peel off, and we love dipping the flesh of the petals into mayonnaise or salad dressing before we dive into the artichoke heart.

Artichokes are very easy to grow. Due to their wild nature, there is a high diversity among plants grown from seed, and some tend to be spikier than others. Commercially, artichokes are propagated from root cuttings, but for the home gardeners, seeds are easy to find. Sow two seeds in an 8–10 cm (3.2–4 inch) pot, and once germinated, choose the strongest of the two seedlings to transplant. As artichokes grow to be quite large plants, plant them at least 1 metre (3.3 feet) apart.

The plants will usually provide a small harvest in the first year, and about six to ten flower buds in the following years. You can trick the plants into early flowering by letting them think they have passed through a whole year. To do this, sow them inside the house in the middle of winter where the temperatures are warm, at least two months before the last frost date. Once germinated, move them to a semi-protected area outside. Here they will experience cold weather and will think that the upcoming spring is their second year, and provide a better crop.

Artichokes benefit from high levels of fertility and plenty of water; if provided, they will reward you with a bountiful harvest. Keep the plants well watered, to encourage large fruit and keep the plants happy. The plants will die back in autumn, then regrow in winter. To keep the plants tidy, once the foliage dies down, cut it close to ground level. If your winters are freezing and experience hard frosts, cover the plants with a layer of mulch to keep them alive.

The Abundant Garden

Beans

Beans are a member of Fabaceae, the legume family. As with other legumes, bean plants form a symbiotic relationship with mycorrhizal fungi, which helps them sequester nitrogen into nodes, to use during seed development. Beans are considered light feeders and contribute to the soil rather than deplete it; still, providing them with fertile soil will increase their yield. There are many hundreds of bean varieties to choose from and they are very versatile in cooking: they can be eaten fresh as young beans or left to mature and dry on the plant, blanched, sautéed, steamed, baked and boiled in soups and stews.

Most beans like to grow in warm weather and don't tolerate frosts. They can be sown directly into the soil, as the seeds are large, easy to handle and germinate quickly. If you have available garden-bed space and adequate growing conditions, beans will benefit from the minimal root disturbance of direct seeding.

Beans can also be seeded into trays and transplanted within two weeks, which is especially helpful if you have an issue with rodents or birds eating the seeds from the beds. This is also useful in very wet weather when the seeds can rot. Soaking the seeds for an hour or two in a large bucket of water will improve their germination rate and give them a head start. If you have mycorrhiza inoculants handy, sprinkle them around the seeds as they are sown in the ground. Keep the soil thoroughly moist while the seeds germinate, which usually takes between seven to twelve days.

Broad beans, also known as fava beans, have been grown and eaten in North Africa, the Middle East and East Asia since 6000–7000 BC. They are the only type of bean that enjoys cold weather and can be sown in autumn or spring. Autumn-sown broad beans grow slowly but they keep the soil covered and the soil biology happy. If chocolate spot (a fungal disease affecting broad beans that looks like brown spots) is affecting your plants, it would be best to grow them in the spring, with adequate spacing to improve air circulation.

Grow broad beans in two rows in the middle of the beds, with plants 10–15 cm (4–6 inches) apart, and sow a few seeds at the end of the bed as replacements in case they are needed. If you

Left Globe artichoke.

Above Broad beans.

grow tall varieties and your site experiences strong wind, you will probably need to support the plants to prevent them from collapsing. Install a few stakes on the bed's perimeter, and tie the plants to the stakes with string.

Common beans and runner beans, which are often grown for their edible pods, were first cultivated in Central America about 2000 BC. Runner beans are perennial and can be dug out at the end of the season, and replanted in the spring. Common beans (either the short bush type or the climbing type, often referred to as pole beans) are annual. Bush beans don't require any support and yield heavily over a week or two. They will produce one main crop, and if allowed to stay in the ground, they will follow up with a second crop several weeks later. For a continuous supply, plant a new succession every two to three weeks. They can be spaced about 5–10 cm (2–4 inches) between plants, in two rows per bed.

Climbing beans will offer a continued harvest over several months and will require trellising. There are lots of options for climbing structures for beans. Several eight-pole teepees with a string looping around the poles will do the job and will be a lovely addition to the garden. Alternatively, stapling wire mesh along the sunny side of a fence or wall works well. Climbing beans make good companions to leafy greens, which utilise the available ground space and enjoy the semi-shaded environment at the base of the plants. Once the leafy greens have been harvested, add another layer of compost to prolong the bean harvest. Space the beans every 10 cm (4 inches) along the fence, or plant two seedlings at the base of every teepee pole. Beans need to be harvested every few days, otherwise they lose their flavour and delicate texture.

Beetroot and chard

Beetroot and chard, also known as silver beet, belong to the Amaranthaceae family. These two vegetables evolved from the same ancestor, but beetroot was bred for its edible root, while chard was bred for its large edible leaves and stalks. All parts of both plants are edible, and they can be harvested at any stage of their growth. Under favourable growing conditions, beetroot

Right Harvesting beetroot.

The Abundant Garden

takes about 10–12 weeks to reach the size of a tennis ball, but the plants can be left in the ground to grow for longer if you prefer a larger size. There are many varieties of beetroot, of various shapes and sizes. We absolutely love yellow beetroots, as their taste is so sweet and full of flavour.

Both chard and beetroot grow year-round and can be either direct seeded into the garden bed or sown into trays. Their seeds are in fact a cluster of smaller seeds stuck together. Germination can be a bit sporadic, therefore transplanting seedlings offers better odds of success. When we sow beetroot seeds into trays, we usually place two seed clusters in each cell to create sets. When we transplant each plug, we discard the weaker one and only plant the most vigorous seedling. We like to plant beetroot in sets of three, 20 cm (8 inches) apart, with a gap of 30 cm (12 inches) between the rows. This spacing provides us with medium-sized beetroots, though if we harvest every second cluster, the remaining plants can grow bigger if left for longer in the bed. You can plant chard with the same spacing but transplant only one plant per planting spot rather than sets. You will get much better results with beetroot and chard if the plants are transplanted at their optimal time; try to avoid letting them sit in their trays for too long.

Beetroot and chard are light feeders, but they will reward you if the soil has a high level of fertility. In our gardens, we need to cover the plants with bird netting or frost cloth from autumn to spring, as birds love to decimate the young leaves. Beetroot makes a good planting companion and can be interplanted around other vegetables, especially since they can be harvested at any stage. Chard plants are gorgeous, especially the rainbow varieties that have brightly coloured crimson, orange or yellow stalks. They are prolific and can be harvested for many months by picking individual leaves.

Broccoli

Broccoli is part of the Brassicaceae family, and is a cultivar of *Brassica oleracea*, the wild cabbage. Many popular vegetables have originated from this plant, including cabbage, cauliflower, Brussels sprouts, collards, and kale. Broccoli is bred and grown for its large flowering head and stalks.

Broccoli is a popular vegetable for good reason; it's nutritious, tasty and versatile. It can be grown year-round, and it benefits from high levels of fertility. There are two main varieties of broccoli: full large heads, and sprouting with many small shoots (known as broccolini). Personally, we prefer the small shoots, as they are ready to harvest in about half the time of the larger heads, yield for a long period and are highly productive.

Be sure to plant the variety that is best for the time of year you are growing it. For a winter harvest, plant broccoli in the autumn. In winter, broccoli grows better with protection, and in summer, it needs constant soil moisture or it will bolt to seed. White butterfly is a typical summertime problem for many brassicas, as it travels long distances to feast on the plants. The best method to control it is to grow the plants under a meshed cloche.

Broccoli is usually grown in trays for four to six weeks, when it is ready to move to the garden. Like all brassicas, plant the stem deep, up to the first true leaves, to help the plant support its weight. The plants grow slowly, but get to be relatively large, and can easily grow to 50 cm (20 inches) in diameter. Plant them in two rows, diagonally spaced, 50 cm (20 inches) apart in the row. Leave the plants after you cut the main stem, as new shoots will still grow afterwards. With broccolini, you will be able to harvest weekly over several months.

Although broccoli and other brassicas benefit from being grown in soil with high levels of fertility, they do not interact with mycorrhiza fungi. Broccoli grow slowly so are suited to interplanting, as many short- or medium-term crops can grow between the plants and get to maturity before the broccoli needs the whole bed space. These shorter-lived crops can interact, feed and be fed by mycorrhiza, and will help the mycorrhiza flourish in the soil.

Cabbage

Cabbage, like broccoli, is also a cultivar of *Brassica oleracea*. Cabbages have been cultivated for so long that the plant's origin has been lost to history.

Cabbage takes a while to grow, and is a heavy feeder that benefits from growing in a fertile bed. You can grow it year round, with a cloche over it in the summer to protect it from the white butterfly, or plant it out in the open in the autumn and early spring. Harvest the whole head when it reaches your desired size and feels firm to touch, before it starts opening and going to seed. The first outer leaves often need to be discarded to reveal the beautiful layers hidden within. There is something very satisfying about growing cabbage, and it is so versatile in the kitchen. We grow a couple of batches a year specifically for making sauerkraut, and we also enjoy it in salads, stir-fries, soups and stews.

As cabbages can take four to five months to grow to maturity from seed, it makes sense to propagate them in trays so the first month or so of growth isn't occupying ground space. Once it is planted, cabbage lends itself to interplanting, for about two months until it needs the extra space. Large-sized cabbage plants will need to be planted 50 cm (20 inches) apart in two rows, whereas smaller varieties can be planted 35–40 cm (14–16 inches) apart in all directions.

Capsicum and chilli peppers

Capsicums, also known as sweet peppers, are warmth-loving plants from the Solanaceae family, which originated in South America. Capsicums are sensitive to the cold, although chilli peppers can withstand a slightly colder temperature range but still prefer warm weather. They can be sown into trays in the spring, but only planted once the risk of frosts passes. Germinate the seeds close together and prick them out to 8 cm (3.2 inch) pots to grow for another month or so. The plants take around five to six months to start yielding fruit from sowing.

Once capsicums do start to produce, around the middle to the

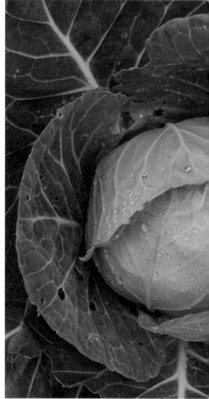

end of summer, they tend to be prolific and will produce well into the autumn. Some varieties grow quite tall and will require support by staking or trellising. Varieties vary in size, and plants can be spaced 30–45 cm (12–18 inches) apart. As capsicum take a while to grow, they can be interplanted with various vegetables, especially the larger varieties.

Capsicums benefit from growing in soil with high levels of fertility and consistent soil-moisture levels. As they stay in the ground for many months, the yield will be greatly improved if you apply additional compost around the plants once flowering starts. You can harvest the fruit early or wait for it to fully mature.

Carrots

Carrots are one of the best vegetables to grow in the garden, as they are absolutely delicious when eaten fresh out of the ground, almost everybody loves them and they are high yielding.

Carrots originated in Central Asia, and are part of the Apiaceae family, along with parsley, celery, fennel, coriander and many other aromatic herbs and vegetables. This family of plants is also known as Umbelliferae because of the plants' inflorescence (cluster of flowers on a stem) forming an umbrella-like arrangement, which makes this family easy to identify.

Many gardeners find carrots hard to grow, as the seeds can take up to three weeks to germinate in cold soil. While carrots can grow year-round, it is much easier to grow them successfully in late spring and early autumn, when they germinate in about 10 days, and there is lower pest pressure from slugs and snails.

There are a few things to watch out for when growing carrots; the most important is to keep the ground constantly moist while they germinate, to use fresh seeds, and to help them survive the onslaught of slugs and snails.

Carrots are best direct-sown into the ground, as the taproot can get damaged if transplanted and result in deformed or stunted carrots. Our preferred way to sow carrots is to sprinkle the seeds lightly in rows every 15 cm (6 inches), aiming for a seed to drop every 2 cm (0.8 inch) or so. With these spacings,

Left Capsicum seedlings

Below Green cabbage.

The Abundant Garden

we have never needed to thin our carrots; if you sow them too closely, you can thin them at the 'baby carrot' stage and enjoy eating them like that.

Carrots are best grown in loose, fertile soil, so they can easily form straight roots. We find that they grow well with or without a compost application at the sowing stage. Avoid any feed that is high in nitrogen, as this will cause excessive leaf growth. Carrots are best sown in weed-free beds. If there is high weed pressure in your garden, you will benefit from using the stale-bed technique (see chapter 6) and early weeding.

Making clear furrows to indicate where the seeds have been sown will help to identify the germinating seedlings, as will covering the seeds with weed-free compost, which will also reduce weeds popping out. Carrots can be interplanted with upright quick-growing crops, such as radishes and turnips, in rows between each row of carrots. If you find gaps in the bed from uneven germination, beets can fill that space nicely.

In summer, it is crucial to have consistent moisture conditions. Cover the bed with a frost cloth or shade cloth on the ground, or with hoops and mesh cover. Make sure to regularly water the germinated seeds, so they never dry out. We tend to sow carrot seeds in deep furrows, so they have access to moisture.

Carrots can be ready to harvest as soon as 60 days after sowing in summer, and as late as 120 days when sown in autumn. When harvesting carrots, avoid breaking the tops when pulling them out; first loosening the soil around the roots by forking. We prefer to pick fresh carrots to eat each day. However, if all the carrots in a bed have reached a good size, and we want to plant another crop in that bed, we will harvest the whole lot and store them. Carrots will store well in the fridge for a month or two if you remove their green tops.

Our favourite carrot variety is 'Scarlet Nantes', which produces tasty carrots that are ready to eat at any stage. This variety also has lots of foliage, which helps to suppress weeds.

Left Niva harvesting carrots.

The Abundant Garden

Corn

Fresh sweetcorn is a lovely treat, and the plants produce lots of biomass for making compost. Corn belongs to the grass family, Poaceae. It was domesticated around 9000 years ago in South Mexico where it became a staple and an important cultural crop. It then spread to both South and North America, where it also became a major crop.

Corn seeds can be sown directly into the ground or transplanted into the garden within about two weeks from sowing into trays. Corn plants are wind pollinated and are best grown in a cluster rather than a long bed, as the pollen spreads better that way. Plants should be spaced about 30 cm (12 inches) apart in all directions.

Corn plants benefit from biologically active soil and high levels of fertility, and will produce more cobs from a single plant as a result. However, even with a good crop, the plants produce a relatively small yield compared to other crops grown in the same area over a similar amount of time. This makes them more suitable for larger gardens or very enthusiastic corn lovers.

To grow a good supply of sweetcorn, sow three to four batches in succession, starting in late spring until mid-summer. Harvest sweetcorn by twisting it off the stalks once the corn silks are dry and have turned brown.

Courgettes

Growing courgettes (*Cucurbita pepo*), also known as zucchini and summer squash, is quite an adventure, as they are incredibly prolific plants. The joke is that one plant will provide enough produce for a household, but you need two for pollination. The courgette originated in Mesoamerica as a type of squash, but the immature green vegetable we recognise today was likely bred in Italy around the nineteenth century.

Sow one seed into an 8–10 cm (3.2–4 inch) pot, about four weeks before the last expected frost date. Typically, courgette plants grow to about 1 metre (3.3 feet) in diameter and should therefore be planted about 1 metre (3.3 feet) apart. When the

Left above Two successions of sweet corn in Harry's garden.

Left below Scallopini.

courgette plants are happy, they will continue growing; some of our plants kept growing until they were 3 metres long! We direct them to where we want them to grow by gently lifting them and removing the older leaves when they are spent.

Courgette plants benefit from a deeply aerated, well-composted bed, and drip irrigation to keep their leaves dry. When you grow courgettes, you are committing yourself to harvesting them almost every day, as the fruit very quickly become oversized. Although oversized courgettes, known as marrows, are edible, they are not as tasty (they are quite nice to eat when grilled). Luckily, courgettes are very versatile in the kitchen, and you can enjoy them raw in salads, sautéed, cooked in soups and stews, braised, fried, grilled, and made into patties, bread, cakes and jams. They are at their best for eating when they are 15–20 cm (6–8 inches) long, so don't let them get away on you.

Harvest courgettes with a sharp knife, leaving at least 0.5 cm (0.2 inches) of the stem, or carefully twist them and hope the fruit doesn't break. The fruit is easily bruised, and the plants are annoyingly scratchy, so you might want to wear gloves and long sleeves when harvesting them.

If you are looking for a change from courgettes, you might want to grow scallopini, which is basically the same in every way except for their spaceship-style fruit and slightly more delicate flavour.

Cucumbers

Cucumbers (*Cucumis sativus*) are our household's favourite vegetable. Native to India, they have been cultivated for over 3000 years, and are popular in Indian cuisine. Cucumbers spread west from India through trading and were grown extensively in the ancient Middle East, appearing in ancient texts across the region. Later they were much celebrated by the Romans, who further spread them across their empire.

We eat cucumbers straight from the vine throughout their growing season, which is from late spring into autumn. We have tried many varieties, and our conclusion is that Lebanese

Above Cucumber seedling.

Below Lebanese cucumbers.

The Abundant Garden

cucumbers produce the best flavour by far, and can be eaten with the thin skin, which doesn't require peeling. The only other competitor for taste is the 'snake melon', which is hard to find and much less disease-resistant than the Lebanese cucumber.

Although Lebanese cucumbers can grow to be large fruits, they are much tastier eaten before they swell up. Their ideal length depends on the cultivar, and ranges between 10–20 cm (4–8 inches), but all are best eaten while they are still skinny.

We germinate cucumbers at the end of winter, sowing them in 8 cm (3.2 inch) pots. We then plant them under cloches, and hope there is not going to be a hard frost. Although the plants can provide fruit for many months, the quality and quantity decline over time. We really enjoy our cucumbers, so to avoid interruptions to our supply, we plant a new succession every eight to ten weeks until the middle of summer.

We grow cucumbers on the ground, letting them sprawl over the bed, but they can be trellised, which will reward you with straighter fruit, because they hang. If not trellised, when the plants reach for the path, gently move the plant back into the bed. We prefer to plant them about 30–35 cm (12–14 inches) apart, diagonally spaced in two rows. Although a bit tight, this spacing provides a high yield without compromising plant health for the first two months of fruiting.

Cucumber plants benefit greatly from a deeply aerated, well-composted bed, and drip irrigation to keep their leaves dry. In the spring, they can be interplanted with fast-maturing crops to utilise the spaces at the edge of the bed. We like to companion plant cucumbers with one sunflower for every six cucumber plants. The sunflowers provide partial shade for the cucumbers during the hot summer days and a plant to climb on, which the cucumbers enjoy. Harvest cucumbers in the cooler hours of the day, using a knife, secateurs or by plucking carefully (be careful not to pull out the whole plant). If you harvest more than you plan to eat immediately, refrigerate the cucumbers as soon as possible.

Above Edible flowers — alyssum, borage, calendula, dianthus, geranium rose, bok choy, coriander and viola.

The Abundant Garden

Edible flowers

Edible flowers are a wonderful addition to a vegetable garden. They are very nutritious and make a lovely addition to salads, drinks and cakes. They can be frozen in ice cubes, added to kids' play potions, and they also attract beneficial insects. There are many edible flower varieties to choose from; some of our favourites include alyssum, borage, calendula, cornflower, dianthus, nasturtium, pineapple sage and viola (pansy).

Most of these plants will not want to leave your garden once they are introduced. Don't say we didn't warn you! It's not that bad, as they can easily be weeded or moved to another section, but if you want to keep them contained, you might want to plant them in a separate bed or around fruit trees.

Most edible flowers are annuals that flower from spring into autumn, though you will likely need two successions to keep them flowering through the season. To prolong their life, harvest them regularly and clear any old flowers to prevent them from going to seed.

Endive and chicory

There are two species of the *Cichorium* genus grown for food: *Cichorium endivia*, which includes curly endive and escarole (broad-leaved endive), and *Cichorium intybus* or common chicory, which is mainly cultivated for its roots and used as a coffee substitute. Leafy varieties of common chicory include radicchio, witloof and sugarloaf. All chicories and endives prefer cooler weather, tolerate frosts, and are fantastic winter greens. Unlike lettuce, they can grow outdoors over winter without any covers. Our favourite variety is frilly endive.

Grow endives and chicories in trays and transplant at around four to five weeks, 20 cm (8 inches) apart. They are light feeders and are generally trouble-free. With frilly endive and escarole, if you harvest just above soil level, the plants will keep growing new leaves and provide you with multiple cuts. Alternatively, you can continuously harvest the outer leaves. Enjoy the leaves while they are still tender and glossy, before they get big and rough.

Fennel

Fennel is an aromatic plant from the Umbelliferae or Apiaceae family, grown for its anise-like flavour. Florence fennel is the cultivar group that forms a delicious bulb that is eaten as a vegetable.

Fennel is our household's second favourite vegetable (after cucumber, and tied with salad turnips). Our daughters snack on the leaves and stems daily. The plants are subtly aromatic and satisfyingly crunchy, and the bulb is excellent in salads, stir-fries, soups and slow-cooked stews.

Fennel is a hardy vegetable and can be grown year-round, without a cover, sown directly in the garden or into trays. For small bulbs, plant 10–15 cm (4–6 inches) apart; for large bulbs 20 cm (8 inches). They can be harvested by cutting off the bulbs at ground level, which will result in multiple new bulbs growing out of the base of the plants. We usually pull out the plants after the second harvest, as the plants can develop large, stubborn root systems that are hard to remove if left in the ground too long.

Some say fennel is an antagonist to most vegetables; we have never noticed any problems but just to be on the safe side we tend to plant it in clusters, rather than interplanting.

Above Florence fennel.

Right Lily harvesting fennel.

Garlic

Garlic is an important member of the *Allium* genus, native to Central Asia. It has been cultivated by humans for many thousands of years, both for its pungent flavour and medicine.

Garlic bulbs are a satisfying vegetable to grow, as you can enjoy them on a daily basis in your kitchen. To grow garlic, choose the largest cloves, as there is a direct correlation between the clove size to the bulb size. Different garlic varieties respond strongly to different soils, and you would benefit from trialling several varieties to see which one works better in your garden.

Garlic is traditionally planted around the shortest day of the year, but since rust has become a major challenge to organic garlic growers in Aotearoa New Zealand, it is best to plant the cloves in

The Abundant Garden

Vegetables

early autumn, so the plants are well established before the rust sets in. You can also increase the spacing between the plants and keep the crop weed-free, to improve ventilation and avoid stagnant air pockets. Our recommended spacing is 15–20 cm (6–8 inches) apart in all directions. Soaking the cloves in compost tea or another microbial rich liquid for a few hours prior to planting will help inoculate the cloves and lead to better plant growth.

Garlic responds well to high soil fertility, mulching and regular foliar sprays. Around the longest day of the year, the foliage will die down and the bulbs will be ready to harvest. That is the time to stop watering and let the ground dry, as frequent watering encourages the garlic to sprout. Once harvested, let the bulbs dry away from direct sunlight, in a well-ventilated area for a week or two before storing in a cool, dry place. The bulbs' tops can be plaited, or the tops can be trimmed and the bulbs stored in a mesh bag.

Jerusalem artichoke

Jerusalem artichoke (*Helianthus tuberosus*) is an extremely flavourful perennial root vegetable. Interestingly it's not a true artichoke nor is it from Jerusalem. Rather, it's part of the sunflower genus, and originates from Eastern North America. The tubers are delicious and have a sweet flavour because of their high inulin content. We especially like Jerusalem artichokes cooked with other root vegetables and blended to make a creamy winter soup. Jerusalem artichokes are considered prebiotic, which means they help feed beneficial gut bacteria.

We don't recommend growing this vegetable in a garden bed, but rather around the garden's perimeter, along fence lines or between fruit trees. It's one of those plants that won't ever go away once established, even if you think you have harvested all the root tubers!

You only need to plant a small piece of the tuber. The plants grow over the warmer part of the year and are ready to harvest in autumn, by forking the ground and digging out the tubers. After harvest, mulch the area to suppress the weeds and allow the plants to grow uninterrupted in the spring. Besides keeping the ground weed free and the ground relatively moist, Jerusalem artichokes don't need any particular care and attention to produce a bountiful harvest.

Kale

Kale is another cultivar of *Brassica oleracea*. It has had a resurgence in popularity in the last two decades for its dark nutritious leaves, which vary in size, colour and shape depending on the variety. However, kale has been an important crop for thousands of years, originating in the Eastern Mediterranean and Asia Minor.

If you are growing kale for its baby leaves, sow it directly in the garden. If desired, the occasional plant can be left to grow to full size, which is about 30 cm (12 inches) in diameter. Alternatively, you can sow seeds into trays and later transplant them into the garden at 30 cm (12 inch) spacings. Plants can grow year-round, though in the summer, they will attract white butterflies, and will need the protection of a mesh covering.

As kale plants take time to reach full size, they lend themselves to interplanting with quick-growing annuals. The plants can grow for close to a year and keep on producing. Once they grow tall, space for interplanting becomes available again under their canopy. Once this occurs, spread a layer of compost and plant into that space. For a continuous harvest pick the outer leaves to eat.

Kohlrabi

Kohlrabi literally means 'cabbage turnip' in German. It is a lovely vegetable from the Brassicaceae family and is another cultivar of *Brassica oleracea*. It is prized for the flesh of its tender, swollen stem, which is juicy and crunchy when eaten raw. Kohlrabi leaves are also edible. There are green and purple-coloured varieties, which are all pale green on the inside when peeled.

Kohlrabi can be sown directly into the bed or into trays to be transplanted into the garden. Plants can be harvested when

The Abundant Garden

small after six weeks from planting or left for 10 to 12 weeks to grow bigger. Plants can be spaced 12–15 cm (4.8–6 inches) apart if harvested small, and 20 cm (8 inches) if allowed to grow bigger. Watch out you don't leave them too long, as they are inedible once they become stringy and tough.

Kūmara

Kūmara (*Ipomoea batatas*, also known as sweet potato or yam) is a spreading vine. It is a staple food for many cultures, as its tubers are sweet and nourishing. Originally from Central or South America where it was first cultivated more than 5000 years ago, it has spread across the Pacific, from island to island, arriving in Aotearoa as an important food crop for Māori. It is a warm-season crop and is best grown in a sunny, sheltered location.

We enjoy growing a patch of kūmara every year, but it is a significant investment, as plants take the whole summer to grow. In fact, it takes the plants a full five months of warm weather to develop tubers, so mark the planting date on your calendar. To propagate your own shoots (tupu), take a box or crate with drainage holes and fill it with sand or pumice. About two months before the last expected frost date, plant tubers with a small gap between them, about 5 cm (2 inches) deep. We prefer to use medium- to large-sized organic tubers, but any tubers with a sprout showing will do. Place the crate in a warm spot to encourage the shoots to germinate. Don't water the tubers at all until shoots start to pop out or they will rot. Once the shoots are 15 cm (6 inches) or so, cut or snap them from the tuber and plant them in the garden, or keep them in a jar with water to encourage even more roots to form. Place the tuber back, as it will grow a second flush of shoots.

Kūmara grows in a wide range of soils but prefers good drainage. Unless your drainage is poor, avoid deep digging, as this will encourage thin tubers. Traditionally, kūmara is planted in small mounds, about 25 cm (10 inches) high, over a hard layer of soil. Plant the shoots 30 cm (12 inches) apart, in two rows, and make sure to keep them well watered for a few weeks until they get established. It is best to plant the flexible shoots by laying them

Left above Young kale.

Left below Kohlrabi.

in a J shape in the ground with the shoot tip pointing upwards, to encourage the tubers to form at the top layer of soil (unlike other roots which we wish to help reach down). The J shape also keeps the roots, in the warmest part of the soil, helping the plant grow faster. Bury most of the shoot, removing any leaves that will be buried, so only the top few leaves poke out of the ground. Keep the bed weed-free until the kūmara has taken over the entire bed and fends for itself.

Check the tubers five months after planting by digging out one plant. If you are happy with the size, you can harvest the whole crop, otherwise leave them for a few more weeks, especially if the summer was a bit cooler than usual. In any case, it is best to dig them all up before a frost is imminent or the ground becomes saturated with prolonged rain, which will cause rot. Ideally, dig them up after a few days of sunny weather. Fork the ground around the plants, being careful not to damage the roots. Lift the tubers out of the ground, treating them gently, like eggs.

Once harvested, kūmara are best cured in the sun or under cover in a well-ventilated place for about a week, to reduce their moisture content and help them develop a hard skin. We keep them in front of the house, because if we leave them on the garden bed, the birds tend to make holes and hollow them out. Don't wash them before storing them; wrap them in newspaper inside a crate or box, and place them in a dry, cool place, away from light and moisture. Any split tubers and the very small and the very large tubers should be eaten first, as they won't store well. If you have more kūmara than you can eat, you can blanch them in boiling water for a few minutes then freeze them.

Leek

Leeks are a flavourful hardy vegetable from the Allium family, prized for their swollen white stems. Leeks can be grown year-round, with suitable varieties for the winter or summer season. The key to successful growing of leeks is to transplant the long seedlings deep in the soil, so only the top few centimetres peek out. Planting deeply encourages the formation of a longer white

Above Planting kūmara in a 'J' shape.

Below Kūmara leaves.

Right Niva harvesting leeks.

stem. Make the planting holes by poking the handle of a rake deep into the ground. An alternative way to increase the amount of white tender stem is to mound soil around the base of the plants as they are growing, but that is considerably more work than planting them deeper.

Propagate leeks in a large deep tray, and mix in plenty of rock dust, as the seedlings will stay in the tray for about 10 to 12 weeks. Make small furrows in the tray, about 5 cm (2 inches) apart, and spread the seeds about 0.5 cm (0.2 inches) apart in the row. Once they are about 15 cm (6 inches) tall, transplant the plants into the growing bed. Space the leeks 15–20 cm (6–8 inches) apart in three or four rows, giving them more space if you intend to leave them until they fully mature. Leeks prefer growing in loose soil with constant high soil-moisture levels. Leeks benefit from high levels of fertility. When harvesting, use a fork to loosen the ground before carefully pulling the leeks out so they don't break. Wash leeks thoroughly before using them in the kitchen to remove any soil particles. The green leaves are also edible, and we enjoy them in soups, stews and stir-fries.

Lettuce

Lettuce is part of the Asteraceae family, originally cultivated by ancient Egyptians, who started the process of breeding the bitterness out of the leaves. Today there is a large variety of lettuces available, in different colours, leaf shapes and forms, from loose heads that make a sweet, crunchy salad, to cos leaves that can act as a platter and be used as a wrap. We grow lots of lettuce, and always have salad dressing on hand to complement it.

Although lettuce can be grown year-round, it is easiest to grow in the spring and autumn. In the hot summer, lettuce needs to be kept well-watered, and sometimes even partly shaded, to reduce the intense summer heat. In the winter, it is too cold and wet for most lettuces (except cos), and it needs to be covered to grow well.

The most common way to grow lettuce is to sow the seeds into trays and plant them four to six weeks later into a fertile bed. For small heads, space the seedlings 15–20 cm (6–8 inches) apart,

Right Red and green frisée lettuces.

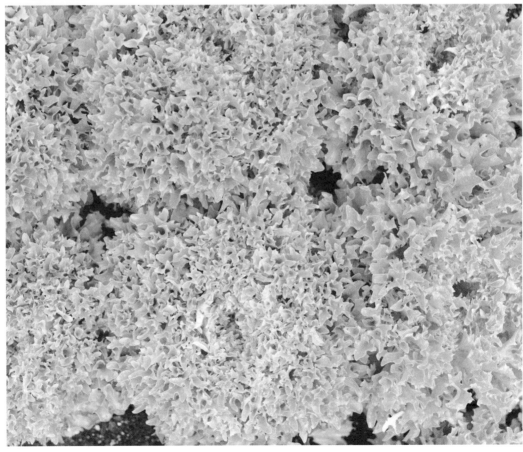

and for larger heads 30 cm (12 inches) apart. Lettuce is a tough plant and a light feeder, so it doesn't need much pampering. Even the plants we discard on the hard path because we think they are too weak to plant, can grow to be beautiful full-grown lettuces almost like the lettuces in the garden bed. An alternative way to grow lettuce is to directly sow it, just like other salad greens, in a shallow furrow, aiming to sprinkle the seeds every 2–3 cm (0.8–1.2 inches) apart within the row, leaving 10 cm (4 inches) between the rows.

Lettuce is a great companion in the garden and can be planted around other large vegetables that don't need the whole bed space while they are young. Interplanting lettuce can also provide them with partial shade during the hot summer.

You can harvest lettuce by cutting the outside leaves, the whole head, or at 3–5 cm (1.2–2 inches) above ground level to allow the lettuce to regrow from the base of the plant for a second, third and sometimes even a fourth cut.

Miner's lettuce

Miner's lettuce, also known as Claytonia (*Claytonia perfoliata*), is native to North America where it mainly grows wild, especially in California. It is a wonderful little green that is sweet and just melts in your mouth. It is easy to grow, and if left to seed, it will provide an endless supply of fresh greens year after year.

The tiny seeds can be directly sown into the beds, into shallow furrows, about 20 cm (8 inches) apart. Once established, they can take over and have little competition from weeds. They are a light feeder and only need the soil to be moist. To harvest, cut the outer leaves or the whole head a few centimetres above ground level.

Mustard greens and rocket

We include many greens of various genus in the Brassicaceae family, including bok choy, Chinese cabbage, cress, mibuna, mizuna, mustard leaves, rocket (arugula), tatsoi and many more. They are mostly grown in the garden in a similar way, and are very adaptable, as they can be harvested as baby leaves or left growing to become large herbaceous plants. These plants can grow year-round and are best sown and planted in spring and autumn. Their pungency and mustardy flavour vary between the cultivars and tend to intensify in warm weather.

Mustard greens and rocket can be sown directly into the beds or into a tray to be later transplanted into the garden. They can be spaced closely, about 1.5–2.5 cm (0.6–inches) apart in rows 5–10 cm (2–4 inches) apart, for harvesting when small as 'cut and come again greens', or planted 15–20 cm (6–8 inches) apart for harvesting large leaves. You can mix varieties together, plant them in clusters of their own or interplanted with other crops, as these quick-growing plants can fill up the available bed space before the main crop needs it.

Onions and spring onions

We use onions (*Allium cepa*) every day in our kitchen, and we take pride in growing our year's supply in the garden.

The best time to sow onions is a month or so after the shortest day of the year. Propagate the onions in a large deep tray, and mix in plenty of extra nutrition with the potting mix, such as rock dust, as the onion seedlings will stay in the tray for about 10 to 12 weeks. Make small furrows in the tray, about 5 cm (2 inches) apart, and spread the seeds about 0.5 cm (0.2 inches) apart in the row. The seedlings are ready to be transplanted when they are as thick as a pencil lead. If your beds have very low weed pressure, and you have the space, you can directly sow the onions straight into the growing bed.

We like our onions to be big, so we plant our onions 15 cm (6 inches) apart in all directions, about 40 onions per square metre

Above Mustard green 'mizuna red coral'.

Below Miner's lettuce.

The Abundant Garden

(10.7 square feet). To plant 365 onions, it takes about 9 square metres (97 square feet) of growing area. If you like your onions smaller, you can plant them 10 cm (4 inches) in every direction. Some years we plant our onions in sets of three, keeping the same number of plants, but planting three plants in one spot, to make planting and weeding easier. When planting, discard the thinner seedlings, as they are most likely to not produce well and are not worth the garden space.

Onions are light feeders and are best planted with no added nitrogen, as it weakens the plants and makes them more appealing to pests. Once the onions are ready to harvest (when they start to dry and the foliage wilts, around the longest day of the year), withhold irrigation from the bed. Once the onions can be pulled with minimal effort, it is time to take them out. Curing (drying out) the onions to reduce their moisture content will help improve their storage ability. Cure them on the bed, using the top to shade the bulbs, or move them to a dry, well-ventilated spot around your house. After a week or so, they can be plaited or trimmed and hung in a sack, in a dry, cool, dark place.

Spring onions are the young plants of various Allium species, and are also known as scallions. As their name suggests, they are best planted or sown during spring, and should be eaten at the time of year onions in storage start to sprout, and before the next crop is ready for harvest. Sow them directly into the garden 1–2 cm (0.4–0.8 inches) apart, with rows 10–15 cm (4–6 inches) apart. Alternatively, they can be sown into trays in clusters of four to six seeds, to be planted together 10 cm (4 inches) apart in all directions. To harvest spring onions, first fork to loosen the ground before carefully pulling them out.

Peas

Peas are part of the Fabaceae or Legume family. Originally from the Mediterranean basin, they have been cultivated since the late Stone Age!

Peas can be divided into shelling peas and snow peas, and there are many varieties of both types. Peas grow well during the cooler

Left above Curing onions for storage.

Left below Spring onion.

months of the year. Shelling peas as their name suggests need to be shelled, and can be eaten fresh or dried and cooked. Snow peas can be eaten in the pod, and the better varieties are stringless and can be eaten both young or more developed.

Peas can be either direct seeded into the garden or can be sown into trays and transplanted within two to three weeks. Pea varieties come in various heights, from dwarf peas that are self-supporting to 2 metre (6.6 foot) tall plants that need trellising, and every possible height in between. There are many options for trellising, including teepee poles, or wire mesh connected to stakes or against a wall. Climbing varieties can be planted or sown 7.5 cm (3 inches) apart in one line along the trellis, and dwarf varieties can be planted or sown 7.5 cm (3 inches) apart in all directions. If mice or birds eat your direct-sowed seeds, then planting seedlings would be a safer option. Be careful that the plants don't suffer from transplanting shock, as that will make them sitting targets for slugs and snails.

About three weeks from when the flowers start to set, you will be able to start harvesting pods. Peas are best eaten fresh after they are picked. Regular picking encourages more flowers and more peas, so visit your pea plants often.

Potatoes

Potatoes are members of the Solanaceae or nightshade family. Potatoes were first cultivated in the areas of southern Peru and north-western Bolivia around 8000 years ago. There are thousands of varieties of potatoes, belonging to several species, with as many as 3000 varieties found in the Andes alone, where potatoes are an essential staple.

Growing potatoes is a rewarding activity. In warm regions, they can grow year-round, but they are mostly treated as a warm-weather crop, as they are frost-sensitive. There are many varieties of potatoes, in many shapes, flavours, textures and colours. Potatoes are generally divided into two categories, early season and main season. The early-season potatoes mature quickly, as fast as two months from planting, and are as prolific as main-season potatoes. Unfortunately they only keep for a couple of months and they

generally have a mild flavour. Main-season potatoes take 100–120 days to mature, and once harvested, they tend to keep for six to nine months.

Although you can plant any potato that starts to sprout, it is the safest to plant certified seed potato that is disease-free. Most garden centres will have these little tubers available, and in some countries, you also have access to certified organic seed potatoes by mail order. Prior to planting the potato tubers, it is best to help them sprout, a practice referred to as chitting. To chit your potatoes, place them in an egg carton or on a tray in a cool, lit room. Place the eyes (little dimples in the flesh) facing up, and small dense sprouts will emerge within a few weeks, increasing yield and giving the plants a head start. It is good practice to chit potatoes, but it's not essential, so don't worry if you don't get it to work. Once the shoots are 1–2 cm (0.4–0.8 inches) long, they can be planted.

Potatoes are hardy plants that are relatively unusual in the vegetable landscape. They are considered soil improvers, but they are also heavy feeders and yield better in fertile soil. To plant potatoes, dig a furrow about 20–30 cm (8–12 inches) deep, and place one tuber every 25–35 cm (10–14 inches) apart. Closer spacing works best for early potatoes and wider spacing for maincrop potatoes. If you notice any shoots or eyes, place them facing up, otherwise lay the potato onto its side. Cover the potatoes with soil while being careful not to break any shoots that formed if you have chitted the potatoes. Within a few weeks, shoots will start to poke out of the soil.

Once the potato's foliage is 15–20 cm (6–8 inches) tall, move more soil from the path to cover the shoots and leaves, creating a mound on top of the bed (known as 'hilling up'). This encourages additional tuber formation along the stem and ensures the potatoes are kept in dark conditions, which prevents them from becoming green and inedible. When mounding the plants you can cover most of the foliage, leaving the top 5 cm (2 in) or so. Mounding can be repeated once or twice more during the growing season.

An alternative method to mounding is to cover the bed with thick mulch, adding more material as the plants grow. This encourages additional tuber formation along the stem and can be repeated one further time.

Early potatoes can be harvested at any time once the tubers are a decent size. Main-season potatoes should be harvested once the tops have dried. Try to be thorough during harvest and remove all the tubers by careful forking and sorting through the soil. Early potatoes can be left in the ground for up to a month, so you can dig them as needed. Main-season potatoes can stay in the ground for a long time but should be dug out before the ground becomes saturated with winter rains. Don't wash your potatoes after harvest, as they won't store as well. Store only the best potatoes that are intact, in a cool dark place, completely blocked from light, so they don't become green. Check on your treasure box once a month or so, and remove any potatoes that seem mouldy so they don't infect the others.

If your crop is relatively good, with no pest or disease issues, you can grow potatoes in the same garden bed for many years in a row. Tubers that have been accidentally left in the ground from the previous season can grow weakly, attracting pests and diseases that can affect your planted crop, so remove them as they come up.

Pumpkins and squash

Pumpkins and squashes originated in the Americas and were domesticated between 5000 and 10,000 years ago. This diverse group of vegetables belongs to five domesticated species of the genus Cucurbita. Although pumpkins are considered a type of squash, the term 'pumpkin' has no agreed botanical or scientific meaning, and it can be used interchangeably with the word squash and winter squash.

Pumpkins are a group of sprawling plants from the Cucurbits family that likes to grow over summer. There are hundreds of varieties, varying in shape, size, colour, flavour and storability. They are incredibly versatile and can be used in soups, stews, fried, baked, stuffed, in cakes, bread, steamed, mashed and even lacto-fermented and pickled.

There are three main species grown by gardeners: pepo, maxima and moschata. *Cucurbita pepo* cultivars are known for being the earliest to ripen, around the middle of summer. Their storability is relatively low, and they are best eaten within six to eight weeks of harvest. Surprisingly, the courgette is also a *Cucurbita pepo*, but it

Above Red kuri squash.

The Abundant Garden

is eaten when it is 'immature', and therefore doesn't keep at room temperature. Our favourite varieties are acorn squash and delicata, and we occasionally enjoy spaghetti squash for its unique texture. Depending on the variety, most plants should be spaced 30–50 cm (12–20 inches) apart.

Cucurbita maximas are the largest squash, both in terms of fruit size and the size of the vines. They can take up a significant amount of space and are difficult to contain. The plants need the whole summer to grow and develop their fruits, but once harvested, most varieties can keep in storage for many months. Our favourites are 'Buttercup', 'Red Kuri' (quickest to mature, incredibly tasty but only keeps for about three months), and 'Queensland Blue'. Most varieties are only suitable for large gardens, or planting at the edge of the bed and allowing to sprawl on the ground around the beds. Plant them 1 metre (3.3 feet) apart.

Cucurbita moschata are generally more tolerant of hot weather and high humidity than other species. It takes the plants a while to produce mature fruit. Butternuts are our favourite *Cucurbita moschata* by far, and we grow a large crop of them every year that keeps well into the following summer. Our favourite butternut variety is 'Chuck's Winter'. Depending on the variety, most plants should be spaced 50–100 cm (20–40 inches) apart.

All species will have improved growth and yield if planted in fertile beds. You can plant large seeds directly in the soil or into 8–10 cm (3.2–4 inch) pots and transplant them within three to four weeks. Keep the plants well weeded, interplant with quick-growing plants or mulch around the plants as they get established; once they cover the bed, they tend to fend for themselves. Keep the plants well-watered, ideally with drip irrigation. You can direct the plants while they grow, by gently lifting them. We like to companion plant squash with sunflowers, which look great with the plants, and provide a bit of extra shade.

Make sure to harvest the fruit with a bit of stem, which helps seal and protect it. Store squash in a cool dark area and remove any fruit that starts to develop mould. If you only grow one variety from each cultivar, you can save the seeds without the risk of cross-pollination. If you do save seeds, make sure to grow at least 12 plants to keep a healthy level of genetic diversity and plant vigour.

Radish

Radish (*Raphanus sativus*), a member of Brassicaceae family, is one of the quickest-growing vegetables there is, taking about four weeks from sowing to harvest over the summer. As they don't take up much space, they are excellent companions to vegetables that take time to fill the bed. Radishes can grow year-round, but tend to prefer the cooler spring and autumn. Radishes have a spicy mustard flavour and a crunchy texture when eaten raw, and are slightly less spicy when cooked. They are versatile in the kitchen and can be eaten raw, marinated, sautéed, steamed, stir-fried, baked, grilled, in soups and ferments.

Although radishes can be sown in trays, it is preferable to directly sow the seed in the garden, either in rows or scattered across the bed. It can be sown at a high density, with seeds spaced every 2.5 cm (1 inch) apart, in rows about 10–15 cm (4–6 inches) apart. As light feeders, radishes don't need any extra fertility boost, and prefer consistent soil-moisture levels.

You might also like to try growing daikon, a large radish used in kimchi that is common throughout Asia.

Salad turnips

Salad turnip (also known as Tokyo turnip) is a Japanese variety of *Brassica rapa* grown for its young tender white roots.

Salad turnips are the third favourite vegetable in our household. Although they are similar to radish in many ways, salad turnips are milder and sweeter. Our daughters eat them like apples! They are best raw and can be eaten with their skin on or peeled, and with or without the tops. They can also be marinated, sautéed, steamed, stir-fried, baked, grilled, and used in soups and ferments.

The seeds and the foliage are smaller than radish, so you can sow them slightly denser than radishes. They take six weeks or so to reach minimal harvest size, but they can grow to the size of large beets if given the space and left to grow for longer.

Right Radishes and salad turnips.

Vegetables

Strawberries

Garden strawberries (*Fragaria × ananassa*) are a hybrid plant from the rose family, Rosaceae.

Strawberries are a delightful plant to grow, as no store-bought strawberry will be as delicious as a truly ripe, fragrant fruit from your garden. Don't be tempted to harvest immature fruits, as strawberries don't ripen well after picking. Commercially grown strawberries are also heavily sprayed, so opt for organic fruit.

Strawberries are perennial and can be grown for many years, although plants will be less productive after the second year and the fruit size will decrease as the years go by. Be extra generous when building fertility in the soil, as the plants will stay there for a while. Strawberries also do well in containers and gutters, as the plants enjoy the extra air circulation and being grown under cover. For these same reasons, they also benefit from raised beds. Plant strawberries in a sunny, well-ventilated spot, though some shading is fine too. We found that planting and growing strawberries through landscape fabric dramatically improves yields, compared to planting them in organic mulch, probably because the strawberries benefit from the warmer soil.

There are many strawberry varieties, divided into three different types: summer-bearing (long-day), everbearing (short-day), and day-neutral, differentiating by the day-length sensitivity of the plant. Summer-bearing yields the largest strawberries over about a month during summer. Everbearing (short-day) strawberries start producing as soon as there are 12 hours of daylight until mid-summer. Day-neutral strawberry plants produce small fruits, two to three times during the year.

Strawberries are generally sold as living plants in punnets or bare rooted. If you are planting bare-rooted plants, take care to spread the roots well, and not to form a J-shape root structure. To enjoy the best harvest, plant them in late autumn to mid-winter, to let the plants get well established before the spring. Spacing varies depending on the variety; large plants are better spaced 35 cm (14 inches) apart, where smaller varieties can be spaced as close as 15 cm (6 inches) apart. If the springs are wet and cold, plants greatly benefit from the protection of being covered. Depending

Right Camarosa strawberries.

Below Dina picking strawberries.

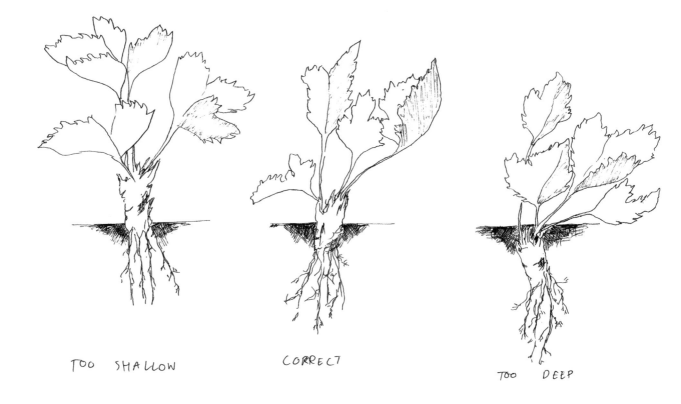

TOO SHALLOW

CORRECT

TOO DEEP

on the bird (or human) pressure you have in your garden, you might want to install hoops over the bed, which you can drape a mesh over to keep the fruits safe. When planting strawberries, pay attention to how deeply you plant the crown.

Strawberries are sensitive to soil-moisture levels, and you should keep the plants well-watered, especially when the plants are flowering and setting fruit. Strawberries are better off irrigated with drip, as when fruits are ripening it is best to keep the plants as dry as possible, to avoid the development of mould. If you see any mouldy fruit, remove them to keep the patch clean.

Strawberry plants need little maintenance, although there are a few things that you can do so that your plants' health and harvest will be greater. Firstly, pick off the flowers the plants produce for the first month or two after planting. This should only be done in the first year, and it helps the plants get better established so that they will yield more fruit for longer. Secondly, foliar spray with seaweed to feed the plants a few times during the season. Thirdly, once the winter colds kick in, cut the plants about 5 cm

(2 inches) above ground level, to remove old foliage and allow the plants to rejuvenate, and thin the clumps to avoid overcrowding in the next season. At this time, you should also take the runners that grow from the plants and use them to create a new patch. The runners are horizontal stems with nodes that grow on the ground, which plants use to clone themselves as a means of reproduction. Installing a new little patch every year will extend the season of your growing harvest, and ensure a fantastic supply of strawberries.

'Camarosa' is our favourite variety, as it has large, firm, fragrant, red-fleshed fruit with excellent flavour. Because it has a high resistance to wet weather, it is ideal in our summers. 'Camarosa' has a vigorous growth habit and is self-fertile; in a good year, you could harvest up to 500 g of the most delicious strawberries from a single plant!

Tomatillo and cape gooseberry

Members of the Solanaceae family, tomatillos (*Physalis philadelphica*) produce edible fruits encased in lantern-shaped husks. Tomatillos are native to Mexico and are a common food in Mesoamerica. Interestingly, fossilised wild tomatillo fruits found in Argentina were dated to 52 million years ago! Tomatillos are the key ingredient in salsa verde and are eaten both raw and cooked. These green fruits are a bit tarter than tomatoes, with a hint of lemony flavour. They are generally picked when the green fruit fills the husk, before they turn pale.

Cape gooseberry (*Physalis peruviana L.*), also known as ground cherry, is a relative of the tomatillo, originating from Peru and Chile. It has smaller and sweeter fruit than the tomatillo and is also encased by a husk. Cape gooseberry is said to grow wherever tomatoes grow and tends to self-seed and spread quickly once established.

Tomatoes

Juicy vine-ripe tomatoes (*Solanum lycopersicum*) are a summer highlight in the vegetable garden. Domesticated initially in Mesoamerica, tomato fruits come in a wide range of colours, shapes, textures and sizes. Tomato plants are divided into determinate and indeterminate categories. Determinate tomato plants have an internal mechanism that tells them to stop growing once they reach a certain size, whereas indeterminate tomatoes can theoretically grow forever! All tomato plants in seed catalogues that need staking to about 1.8 metres (6 feet) are indeterminate. Tomatoes are one of those plants that keep on giving, depending on how much you invest in them. Most home gardeners will achieve an average yield of 1.5 kg (3.3 lb) per plant; commercial growers will aim for 10 times that, while the Guinness world record exceeds a whooping 180 kg (400 lb).

Tomatoes are frost-sensitive, warmth-loving plants, but they can also grow in low temperatures. Start propagating your plants as early as eight weeks before you intend to plant them. Sow the seeds into trays and about two weeks after they germinate, move them into 10 cm (4 inch) pots or larger containers. Remember to add extra fertilisers into these pots, and to bury the seedling up to the first true leaves. Germinate at least 20 per cent more seeds than you need, so you can choose the largest and heaviest seedlings and discard the rest.

Tomato spacings can vary depending on your preferred growing style and trellising system. Dwarf tomatoes can be spaced every 30–40 cm (12–16 inches). Determinate and indeterminate tomatoes can be spaced 30–50 cm (12–20 inches) if trellised, and 50–80 cm (20–32 inches) if planted in a cage or allowed to sprawl on the ground. Trellising systems can be anything sturdy enough to hold the weight of the plants and resist the summer winds that prevail in your area, and it can be as simple as tying the plant up a stake, or a simple bamboo structure as shown in the illustrations. The general rule is that with close spacing between your plants, your yield per plant will be lower, but the overall yield per area will be bigger, and vice versa.

Tomatoes are heavy feeders that greatly benefit from high

Above Cherry tomatoes.

Right above Tomato plant trellised on a stake.

Right below Tomatoes trellised on a frame, and companion planted with basil and marigolds.

The Abundant Garden

Vegetables

levels of fertility, mulch, regular watering through drip irrigation, and regular foliar spraying. The plant's roots systems are relatively shallow, but as they can spread out for several metres once they are mature. During the growing season, we apply a second and sometimes even a third supplemental compost application over the beds, to provide more nutrition to the growing and fruiting plants.

Tomato plants are very vegetative and send lots of side shoots, known as suckers or laterals. Laterals are easy to spot, as they always pop out between the leaf and the stem. When growing determinate plants (usually bushy varieties), don't remove the laterals.

When growing indeterminate plants (usually taller varieties), the question is how many laterals you can support, in terms of the trellising system, space and fertility. We tend to choose one or two strong laterals, and trellis them, as if they were individual plants. All the other laterals get removed by pinching them by hand a bit above their connection to the plant, or if they have already grown over 0.5 cm (0.2 inch) thick, we cut them with a knife. If a lateral already has a fruiting cluster, then you can pinch its growing tip, so it will stop growing but the fruit will ripen. Laterals grow quickly, and it is best to check on your plants once or twice a week for early removal, preferably on sunny days so the plants heal quickly.

As the plant grows taller, remove the bottom leaves below the fruiting truss. This improves the plant's health, and improves air circulation at the base of the plant.

Tomatoes are a common tunnel house crop, as tunnel houses provide a warmer environment and protection from rain and winds. In the tunnel house, you can trellis the plants with strings tied to the frame. In our tunnel house, we use a system called 'lower and lean'; when the plants reach the roof of the structure, we release the string and let the stem of the plants slack on the ground, which lowers the plant and gives it more room to grow. This way, our plants often grow to 6–10 metres (20–30 feet) by the end of the season.

Harvest vine-ripened tomatoes by waiting for them to be fully coloured, but before they over-ripen or split. You can hand-pick tomatoes by breaking the stalk just above the calyx, which keeps a bit of stalk attached to the tomato. Tomatoes can ripen after picking, so if birds are pecking your fruit, don't hesitate to pick them and

Right Yotam trellising and de-lateraling tomatoes.

The Abundant Garden

Vegetables

move them to a safe place at room temperature. Don't refrigerate tomatoes below 10°C (50°F), as they will lose their flavour.

Tomatoes lend themselves to interplanting, as they take a while to fill their bed space, and as they grow vertically, they leave lots of room for low-growing plants. It is best to interplant light feeders that will not compete with the tomato plants. Basil and marigolds are classic companions, but we have had success with many herbs, greens and root vegetables. The trick is to make sure the plants have enough access to light, or they won't grow well.

Watermelon and muskmelon

Watermelons (*Citrullus lanatus*) and muskmelon (*Cucumis melo*), are sprawling members of the Cucurbitaceae family, which grow in warm weather and are frost sensitive. Watermelons are native to and were first cultivated in Africa some 5000 years ago. Watermelons and muskmelons are among the sweetest crops you can grow in the garden. Every year we grow a decent watermelon patch and closely observe their development with much anticipation. There are hundreds of varieties to choose from, and alongside the sweet red watermelons, such as 'Sugar Baby', we love growing the heirloom 'Moon and Stars', as well as yellow-fleshed varieties.

Seeds can be directly sown into the ground once there is no risk of frost or about three weeks earlier into 6–8 cm (2.4–3.2 inch) pots. Although plants grow stems up to 3 metres long that spread in all directions, you can easily direct their growth. You can space the plants 30–45 cm (12–18 inches) apart, in two rows across the bed. If you are sowing them directly into the beds, we suggest slightly closer spacings to compensate for non-germinating seeds.

Watermelons will appreciate the warmest, sunniest part of the garden you can offer them, and they benefit from high levels of fertility and drip irrigation. If your summer season is short, consider planting these plants through weedmat or laying black tarp on the ground around them, and using hoops with clear film to create a warmer environment. As the plants grow slowly in the spring, they lend themselves to interplanting with many quick-growing annuals, and of course, sunflowers.

Above Yacón foliage.

Below Yacón.

The trickiest part when growing watermelons is how to determine if they are ripe. This is actually easier with muskmelons, as they become fragrant once ripe, so yes, the test is to smell the fruit. With watermelons, it's a bit more of an art. The easiest indicator is when the fruit's stem starts to dry out. The other indicator is tapping the fruit to identify a hollow sound that indicates ripeness, but sometimes this will cause you to miss the boat. When you think the fruit is ripe, pick just one. If it is ripe, good news, and if not, you can still eat it and wait patiently for a few more weeks before picking the next one.

Yacón

Yacón (*Smallanthus sonchifolius*) is a member of the Asteraceae family. It is a root vegetable native to the eastern slopes of the Andes, where it can still be found in the wild. It has probably been cultivated for thousands of years. It is a remarkable plant that produces a prolific yield of large translucent tubers with sweet, crunchy flesh that is considered prebiotic. We use it extensively in our kitchen, as it can be peeled and sliced into sticks to be eaten raw, or eaten in stir-fries, soups and stews. Storing the roots for a few weeks after harvest or exposing them to sunlight increases their sweetness.

The plants usually grow from inedible rhizomes (crowns), although they can also be propagated from the edible tubers by planting them in pots and placing them in a warm place. The plants grow to be reasonably large and can reach 2 metres (6.6 feet) tall. They should be planted no closer than 60 cm (24 inches) apart, and about 10 cm (4 inches) deep. The plants should be planted in spring and will take the whole summer to grow the tubers. The edible tubers improve their taste in cold weather and can be kept in the ground as long as the ground drains well and is not saturated. Harvest by forking carefully around the plants. The crown can then be propagated in pots, or immediately planted back into the soil.

Plant yacón in a sunny, free-draining, fertile spot, and keep the plants well watered throughout the season. They are pretty much maintenance-free. As they take time to bulk up, they can be interplanted with many quick-growing annuals.

Other vegetables and herbs

Fresh herbs and greens are some of the best plants to grow in the garden, as they are easy to grow, and their nutritional content is far greater when fresh. Diversify your garden by growing greens from different botanical families throughout the season. Eating a wide range of plants is a culinary delight, and will lead to a healthier diet with an increased range of nutrients.

Asparagus

Asparagus plants can be propagated from seeds or planted as crowns, 45 cm (16 inches) apart. Unlike other vegetables, you will need to let the plants grow for two to three years, depending on the variety, before harvesting the fronds. Plants live for 15 to 25 years, and the edible spears pop out of the ground in the spring. To stagger your harvest over a longer period, plant the crowns at different depths, from 5–20 cm (2–6 inches) deep.

Basil

Plant this warmth-loving aromatic herb 25 cm (10 inches) apart, or in between tomato plants, and pick it regularly to encourage new leaves. Harvest by pinching the tips of the plant, just above where a new set of side shoots is growing. This encourages the plant to keep growing in a bushy shape, and continue to provide fresh leaves over a long season.

Celery and celeriac

These plants benefit from a high level of fertility and need constant soil-moisture levels. Celery needs no introduction. Celeriac has been bred for its enlarged roots, which are highly aromatic and brighten winter soups and stews. Seeds take two to three weeks to germinate, and the plants take three to five months to grow once planted. Space plants 35–45 cm (14–18 inches) apart.

Collard

Collard is a close relative to kale, with large cabbage-like leaves. The leaves are continuously harvested over a long period, and although it can be grown year-round, they are tastier in cold

Above First-year asparagus, grown in a pot.

Below Basil.

weather. Collard leaves can be used the same way as cabbage and kale, and can also be used as raw wraps.

Coriander (cilantro)

This aromatic herb can be directly sown into the garden at close spacings or transplanted as seedlings at 10 cm (4 inches) apart. As coriander is short-lived, keep planting new plants every three to four weeks for a consistent supply.

Corn salad

Also known as claytonia and mâche, corn salad has a nutty flavour and soft green leaves. The plants can be directly sown as baby greens or transplanted individually at 10 cm (4 inch) spacings. Best grown over the colder months of the year, as it tends to bolt in warm weather.

Dill

This aromatic herb grows best from seed and can be spaced 3–5 cm (0.4–0.8 inches) apart in rows. Harvest it regularly by cutting it at the base of the plant. Dill flowers and seeds are also delicious.

Edible weeds

We don't advocate sowing or encouraging edible weeds in the garden, as they tend to take over and make it difficult to grow vegetables. However, if you are 'lucky' to have edible weeds in your gardens, such as chickweed, dandelion, lambs' quarters, plantain and purslane, enjoy them! You can eat them raw in salads, and in smoothies mixed with frozen bananas.

Magenta spreen

With its gorgeous magenta colour, magenta spreen is a less invasive weed than the traditional lambs' quarters, but it is still best to harvest young plants before they spread seeds. When fully grown magenta spreen can reach over 1 metre (3.3 feet) tall. They are extremely nourishing plants with tasty edible leaves, closely related to spinach, and are used extensively in Asia. Like their spinach relatives, they have a high level of oxalic acid in mature leaves, which can be removed by boiling or frying them for a couple of minutes.

Minutina

Minutina is a delicate, nutty, crunchy green that can grow year-round, though is best over the colder months. It is a relative of plantain and is shaped like serrated grass. It is easily grown from seed or as transplants. Plants can be spaced closely and harvested young or given more space and grown the size of small lettuces.

New Zealand spinach

New Zealand spinach isn't from New Zealand and it's not spinach! Also known as tetragonia, it is a hardy, warm-weather green, and is edible when cooked. These plants grow to a relatively large size, so space them 30–40 cm (12–16 inches) apart.

Oca

Also known as New Zealand yam, oca is a non-invasive relative of oxalis, and is prized for its colourful edible tubers and green leaves. Grow oca over the summer like potatoes, including mounding for increased yield.

Orach (mountain spinach)

Orach is a hardy summer green that grows well in warm weather. It makes an attractive salad with its delicate texture and purple and pink varieties. It can grow as a baby leaf or as a tall bush about 1 metre (3.3 feet) high.

Parsley

Parsley can grow year-round. Varieties with flat leaves such as Italian parsley have a better taste, while curly parsley is lovely as a garnish. Transplant new plants every three to four months, about 15 cm (6 inches) apart, for year-round supply.

Parsnip

Parsnip is a root vegetable with distinctly shaped leaves and flavoured cream-coloured roots. It is related to carrots, and is a long-season crop that can take about three weeks to germinate, and four to six months to grow to maturity. Grow parsnips like carrots, but at a larger spacing of about 5 cm (2 inches) between plants. Only use fresh seeds, no older than a year old.

Above Comfrey and za'atar.

Left Oca.

Perennial herbs

Perennial herbs attract pollinators and provide a year-round yield. They can be planted at the edge of garden beds or around the garden, as many of them are hardy, large plants that don't need the comfort of a growing bed. They are best established without weeds around them, but once established, they can live around the lawn, and only need water. We love growing herbs, and use them in cooking, as medicinal herbs or infuse them in near-boiling water for herbal teas. There are many cultivars and varieties to choose from. Thyme, rosemary, hyssop, French tarragon, chamomile, sage, chives, horseradish, marjoram, lemongrass, oregano, lemon verbena, liquorice, lovage, marshmallow, za'atar and sorrel are some of our favourites. Mint and lemon balm should be planted in pots or alongside other hardy herbs to act as a barrier, as otherwise they can spread over large areas.

Spinach

Different varieties of spinach suit different seasons, and with the right choice, spinach can be grown year-round. You can directly sow it in the bed for baby leaf or as transplants for larger, lettuce-sized plants.

Chapter 9
Gardening through the seasons and crop planning

In this chapter, we explore the unique rhythm of the seasons and how to create a garden plan for a year-round harvest. Each season in the garden is different and has its tasks, challenges and opportunities. Ride the waves of the seasonal patterns to avoid being overwhelmed, while getting the most out of your garden.

Autumn and winter

When planning your cropping for the colder seasons, remember that the days-to-maturity (DTM) changes throughout the year. The general rule that applies to all vegetables is that the DTM shortens gradually from late winter to spring, and increases gradually from autumn to winter. As the daylight hours decrease and the weather gets colder in autumn, plants grow more slowly and require more time to reach maturity. In cold climates, this

Right Frost in the gardens.

The Abundant Garden

might even mean plants stop growing altogether, and stay dormant until the weather warms up again. The general rule is that when the grass stops growing, vegetables stop as well.

Most vegetables need to be well established before the cold weather kicks in, as they will not be able to get established in harsh winter conditions. In winter, most crops grow better under cover. Many year-round crops, such as radish, lettuce and many mustard greens, need to be established in autumn to be harvested in winter. If plants are established early enough in autumn, they can keep on growing over winter without any covers. If that planting window has been missed, it is still possible to grow them under hoops and growing cover.

In our wet climate, most lettuce varieties rot in the open ground when planted in winter, but can be grown under a cover. A simple cover such as a woven mesh, which keeps conditions a bit dryer and warmer, will do the trick. Another tip for growing lettuce in winter is to transplant it a little higher than the soil level, to increase the air circulation around the base of the plants. With other crops such as beets and carrots, using covers in winter cuts the DTM in half. The quicker a crop grows, the better the quality of the crop will be.

In winter, most vegetables tend to grow more compactly and take up less space. Since there is also less competition for water at this time, you can slightly increase the planting density to utilise the bed space fully. Growing vegetables in winter is a pleasure, as there is little need to water the plants. On the other hand, weeding becomes more challenging, as most weeds need to be picked up and removed from the garden, otherwise they may re-root themselves. Watch out for dry spells during the spring; plants will bolt to seed early if they are not sufficiently watered.

Spring

Spring is often a happy time for plants, and for gardeners too! The lengthening daylight hours and warmer days send a signal to plants to start growing. In nature, most plants use this time of year to get established while there is still plenty of moisture in the soil.

Above Cucumbers grown in weedmat under plastic film cover.

When we grow summer vegetables, we start by germinating the seeds early, about two months before the last predicted frost. Naturally, summer crops germinate much better in warmer temperatures, so we germinate them inside the house where the room temperature is usually high enough. We sometimes place them near the woodstove for a bit of extra heat, or on a sunny counter. As soon as the first little plants emerge, they need lots of light. A sunny kitchen bench is a good place, or you could move them outdoors in the morning and bring them back inside in the evening.

When growing plants in the early spring, they will benefit from being planted under a cloche, as otherwise conditions out in the open will be too cold and harsh. Even as the frost risk passes, most crops will still benefit from growing under a cover and will grow faster this way.

Try to get most of your main succession of summer crops established by the end of spring, as that helps to create a living mulch. While most plants can still become established in the summer, they will require more watering.

Pay extra attention to weeding in the spring; the weeds are also aware that this is the best time of year to grow, and they will quickly produce viable seeds. Weeding your garden every fortnight will help you get on top of the weeds while they are young, making it a swift and pleasant activity. Try to time your weeding sessions with a few days of sunny weather, and weed in the morning so the weeds won't need to be picked up, but rather can dry out in the hot sun.

Summer

Summer is generally the time most plants produce fruit and seeds. The key to summer growing is simple but important: watering. Adequate soil-moisture levels tell the plants that it is safe to continue growing. Once plants experience a sharp water shortage, they take it as a signal to concentrate all their efforts on reproduction, and will bolt to seed. For most vegetable gardeners, the majority of summer work is to harvest and irrigate. If you

The Abundant Garden

automate or semi-automate your watering system, as we discuss in chapter 7, you can save a significant amount of time.

Reducing atmospheric temperature is also beneficial for better plant growth. When plants get too hot, they stop photosynthesising and instead direct their energy into keeping themselves cool. By covering the bed with a mesh cloche, most year-round vegetables stay cooler and perform better than out in the open. You could also cool plants down in summer by planting them in semi-shaded areas, or by using sprinklers or misters.

Year-round vegetables have a short DTM in summer as plants grow quickly at this time of year. This means that it is best to sow and plant smaller amounts of plants, but more often.

During the summer, long-term crops would benefit from extra love and care. Observe your plants growing, and keep thinking about how you can help them to grow better. Small actions such as removing diseased or sad-looking leaves helps to improve ventilation around the crop and keep them healthier. A second application of compost and regular foliar feeding helps a lot as well. Vine-spreading crops such as cucumbers and squash will go wild unless you direct them where you want them to grow. To keep their harvest manageable, move them out of the path back into the growing bed or trim them back. Tomatoes will need trellising or staking, as well as pruning and de-lateraling. Beans will need a bit of directing onto their trellising.

The end of summer is often referred to as a second spring. Temperatures and daylight levels are still high, and the end-of-season rain brings the garden back to life. *To enjoy a year-round vegetable supply from your garden, this is the time to get back into propagating and planting.* Most plants you put in the ground now will reach maturity quickly, and this is the window to grow more vegetables for ample harvests in the autumn, winter and spring.

Crop rotation

Rotating crops throughout the garden is good practice for two main reasons: firstly, to prevent crop-specific pests and diseases becoming established in the soil, and secondly, to prevent the soil

Left above Peach tree blossom.

Left below Sunset in spring.

204   The Abundant Garden

becoming depleted in minerals specific to a particular crop's needs.

There are other reasons to rotate between crops. Varying between crops and botanical families helps to feed different soil microbes and develop a more robust soil ecology. Some crops, such as vegetables from the legume family and many cover crops, help to enrich the soil and increase microbial activity, to the benefit of the following crop. Some crops are more sensitive to certain soil pests or disease, and growing a thick crop of brassicas or alliums can help to sanitise the soil.

It is best to rotate the main summer crops (cucumber, courgette, eggplant, peppers, onion, garlic, strawberries) so that they have a three-year break before growing in the same place again. As much as feasible, it is best to try to rotate all your crops between the beds and avoid growing two crops from the same botanical family in the same bed in the same season. This is a general guideline and a good practice to keep in mind long-term. However, if you are short of available bed space, and if your first crop of that botanical family grew well, you can grow two crops consecutively without any immediate harmful effects.

In the home garden, it can be difficult to rotate crops. While crop rotation is best practice, it's not the end of the world if you can't manage it in a home garden for a couple of reasons. Firstly, when you make your own compost from your crops, using that compost in the garden helps to distribute minerals more evenly. Also, growing several crops together in the same bed complicates crop rotation. As a general rule, we emphasise crop rotation for crops that stay in the ground for three months or longer. It's less critical to rotate short-term crops or crops grown in small amounts.

Cover crops

Cover crops such as oats, rye, lupins and buckwheat help to mineralise the soil and improve the soil's structure, while cultivating the soil's living community. These crops provide sugars to the microorganisms while they are growing. Their extensive root systems reach deep into the subsoil and draw minerals from

Left above, left Bumblebee enjoying the zinnia flowers.

Left above, right Sunflowers.

Left below A cover crop of lupins.

Above Cover crops.

Left Courgette planted in weedmat under hoop with plastic film cover.

Page 208 Courgettes fruiting in late October.

　　　　The Abundant Garden

lower levels of the soil into their plant material. When they finish growing, regardless of whether they are dug into the ground or pulled out to make compost, the majority of their root system stays in the ground, becoming food for the soil's microorganisms and the plants that follow them.

Most cover crops improve the soil conditions so much that they replace the need to add compost into the growing bed for the next crop. In larger gardens, growing cover crops is a fantastic way to incorporate organic matter and improve the soil fertility. In smaller gardens, it is more sensible to use the precious growing space for growing food. Even if you only have a short growing window of three to six weeks before the next crop goes in the ground, it can be beneficial to sow cover crops rather than leaving the soil bare.

Leguminous cover crops such as lupins, peas and vetch store nitrogen in nodes around their roots through symbiosis with mycorrhizal fungi. The plants will use most of this nitrogen during the flowering and seed development stages, leaving little additional nitrogen in the ground once the crop has finished growing. If you want to keep the nitrogen in the ground for the benefit of the next crop, cut these plants when they are starting to flower. However, if your goal is to grow cover crops for making compost, letting them flower will allow them to develop more complex carbohydrates and provide a more stable carbon source for the compost pile.

When cover crops flower, they add grace to the garden as well as provide food for bees and beneficial insects. Pull the plants out when they're in the sweet spot between their usability in compost-making and enriching the soil, which is when they are well into their flowering stage, but before they set any seeds.

Growing covers

Using covers is a crucial step in being able to grow reliably year-round. With increasing climate disruption, growing under a cover can provide a safer environment for your crops. Plants become stressed when you push them to the edge of their comfort zone; this stress affects their health, yield, quality and flavour. By modifying

The Abundant Garden

Using plastic film covers

From late autumn through winter and early spring, you can cover crops with plastic film, making mini tunnel houses. The soil and air temperature inside the cloche will be warmer than the outside temperature during the day, and plants will respond with faster and healthier growth. Plastic film cloches are better than mesh cloches in this regard. On sunny spring days, open the cloches so that the plants don't get too hot. If there is a period without rain, you can keep the covers half-open, and put them back when rain is forecast. Remove the cloches when the weather conditions are consistently warm enough, or when the plants outgrow their cloche. Plant early summer crops under cloches when there is still the chance of frost. Most plants will grow to be healthy and productive, but a heavy frost can still kill them! Plan for close crop successions in late winter to early spring to be on the safe side, and look for varieties that do well under cold conditions. When planting under plastic film, be aware that the lack of ventilation can lead to trapped moisture and increased disease pressure. To avoid this, don't wrap the film all the way down to create a complete seal; instead, allow for air gaps close to the ground.

the growing environment and growing within the crops' comfort zone, your plants will be healthier, and they can provide you with a higher yield while maintaining excellent flavour.

You can successfully reuse the same covers and fabrics for many years if you invest in high-quality fabrics and films. To prolong their life, store the covers in the shade when they are not in use. You can use bent plastic pipe, metal hoops or wooden frames to create structures that will support your growing cover. In garden locations that experience strong winds, you will need to peg down or add weights, such as rocks, to anchor your structure to keep it in place.

Investing in structures that fit your garden size, from small field cloches to tunnel houses you can stand up in, is well worth the investment if you are committed to using them. Be sure to anchor these structures according to the windiness of your site; consult the supplier if you are unsure.

With structures that use plastic film, the main challenge is ensuring enough ventilation and preventing them from getting too hot during the summer.

Permanent tunnel houses would benefit from having sidewalls with a mesh cover that can be left open in the summer as well as roof vents. If the vents are not enough to prevent overheating, you can place a temporary light shade cloth on top of the tunnel house during the summer to keep conditions favourable for plant growth. The general rule is that if it is uncomfortable for you inside the tunnel house, it is uncomfortable for your plants as well.

Crop planning

With good planning, you can enjoy a wide range of vegetables throughout the year. Your choice of crops will have a big impact on how much work your garden will require.

Crops that grow quickly usually provide a larger yield per area compared to crops that grow over a long period of time. While quick-growing crops don't require more work than other plants to grow, extra work occurs because they are out of the ground faster so the garden bed is cleared and a new crop is planted more often. In our most intensively used beds, we can have up to eight different crops growing in the same bed during a single season.

Long-term crops such as tomatoes, courgettes and cucumbers also require more work during the season, mostly because they need to be frequently harvested. Plant these as close as you can to your house and harvest every other day during their peak production window.

Our recommendation is to plan your garden's size to match what you can manage and aim to keep it in full production of high-yielding crops. When planning succession planting, little and often works best, because the workload is much more manageable and the harvest is evenly spaced.

Sowing plants at their preferred time (and taking care of them properly) will reward you with an abundant, high-quality harvest. Even though many vegetables can grow year-round, often they will grow better and more easily in a particular season. For example, greens and many root vegetables are not easy to establish in mid- to late summer, as they don't like high temperatures and require regular watering and high soil moisture to thrive. Enjoy the summer crops while they last, and sow a new succession of greens and root crops when the rains return. Seasons can be extended, but only within reason, so it is best to concentrate on crops that grow best in their preferred season.

Record keeping and garden mapping

It is useful to keep a schematic map of your garden beds, to plan your garden's vegetable production and crop rotation. The map can be photocopied for repeated use, or copied to another page of your garden diary. Use your garden map to plan ahead and write down which long-term crops are going to go into which bed. Planning ahead will help you reserve precious garden space for the crops you care most about, and be less likely to spontaneously plant something in an otherwise reserved spot.

If you want to take your crop planning to the next level, once you gain an understanding of how long different crops stay in the ground, you can create a table like the one opposite. This way, you can plan ahead and know which crops will follow which.

My garden plan

	Aug	Sept	Oct	Nov	Dec	Jan	Feb	March	April	May	June	July
Bed 1												
Bed 2												
Bed 3												
Bed 4												
Bed 5												
Bed 6												
Bed 7												

Use planners that you make as a guide. It's crucial to allow yourself flexibility around planting, as plants will be ready for harvest at different times depending on the weather. If the space you planned to use for a particular crop is not available, plant it in another spot.

Many crops will continue to yield until their last breath, but the quantity and quality will drop over time. So, while it can be a good idea to allow crops that do well to stay in the garden longer, don't hesitate to remove a crop at the end of its life cycle if you need the space for a new crop planting.

Here are some things to consider when creating your garden plan.

- Only grow vegetables you and your household love and enjoy eating.
- Grow plants according to their seasonal preferences (and limits).
- Grow plants where they will thrive.
- Grow small amounts of plants at a time, followed by future successions. This prevents having to harvest an enormous amount of one crop at once, and provides a harvest over a long period.
- Plan for when you would like to harvest your crops, or if you will be harvesting for a while, when you will start harvesting. Use this information to determine both the plant spacings and how much to grow in each succession.
- Plan for diversity of crops to harvest throughout the year.
- Aim to have plants growing in every square metre of your garden.
- Group plants by watering preferences.
- Grow crops that you are good at growing and which lend themselves to your growing environment. Build upon your successes, repeating and refining growing vegetables that grow well for you and your garden's characteristics.
- Grow crops that you don't want to buy, such as vegetables that are typically heavily sprayed.
- Grow high-yielding vegetable varieties. Some crops offer a better return for the effort of growing them. Concentrate on early-maturing varieties that also taste fantastic.

- Grow high-value vegetables. Some vegetables are more expensive to purchase and growing them can offer a better financial return. Price is not everything, and high-value vegetables are a factor of the yield, price and how long the crop is in the ground.

Crop characteristics

The following crop characteristics will help you to plan which plants to include in your garden planner at what time.

Prolific crops

Beans (climbing), carrots, courgettes, cucumbers, eggplants, kale, leafy greens and herbs, lettuces, microgreens, peas, potatoes, radishes, tomatoes, turnips.

Quick-growing crops

Beans (bush), carrots (summer), cucumbers (summer), courgettes (summer), herbs, lettuces, microgreens, mustard greens, pea, potato (early varieties), radishes, spinach, spring onions, turnips.

Crops that grow well with drip irrigation

Artichoke, basil, beans, beetroot and chard, broccoli, cabbage, capsicum and chilli peppers, celery, corn, courgettes, cucumbers, edible flowers, eggplants, fennel, garlic, kale, kohlrabi, leeks, lettuces, onions, peas, potatoes, pumpkins and squashes, strawberries, tomatoes, tomatillos, yacón, watermelon.

Crops that grow well with sprinkler irrigation

Beetroot and chard, broccoli, cabbage, carrots, celery, chicory, corn, edible flowers, fennel, most herbs, Jerusalem artichokes, kale, kohlrabi, kūmara, leeks, lettuces, mustard greens and rocket, peas, potatoes, radishes, turnips, yacón.

Plants to grow in partial shade (at least 6 hours a day)

Beetroot and chard, endive, fennel, herbs, kale, kohlrabi, lettuces, mustard greens, miner's lettuce, radishes, rocket, spinach, strawberries, turnips.

Propagation calendar

With your garden plan in mind, it is a good idea to create an actionable propagation plan, to help you keep track of what needs doing when. In your calendar, specify when you will sow or purchase each plant.

Garden plant plan

Month	Crop and variety	Number of plants	Tray or pot type	Weeks to transplanting	Spacing in garden bed	Comments
August	Cucumber – Lebanese	4	8cm	4	40cm	Cover bed until harvest begins
	Lettuce – red and green	12	tray	5	25cm	
	Potato – lesieta	18	direct in the garden		30cm in two rows	
	Radish – French breakfast	1 metre row	direct in the garden		2 to 3 cm apart	
	Beets – ace and touchstone	30	tray	4	clusters of 3 every 15cm, in 3 rows	
September						
October						
November						

Vegetable planting chart

The following vegetable planting chart gives you the optimal spacing range and sowing times for popular vegetables.

Choose closer spacings for compact varieties and for harvesting roots and leaves crops at a younger stage, and choose larger spacing for full-sized vegetables and larger varieties. Closer spacings for fruiting crops will increase the overall yield per square metre, while reducing the yield per plant.

Vegetable	Spacings	Planting and sowing times	Botanical family
Artichoke	100 cm (40 inches)	Autumn and winter	Asteraceae
Basil	15–25 cm (6–10 inches)	Spring and summer	Lamiaceae
Bean (broad)	7 cm (3 inches), 30 cm (12 inches) between rows	Spring and summer	Fabaceae
Bean (climbing)	5–10 cm (2–4 inches)	Spring and summer	Fabaceae
Bean (dwarf)	20–30 cm (8–12 inches)	Spring and summer	Fabaceae
Beetroot	20 cm (8 inches) between clusters of 3	Spring to autumn	Amaranthaceae
Broccoli	35–45 cm (14–18 inches)	Spring, autumn	Brassicaceae
Cabbage	35–45 cm (14–18 inches)	Spring, autumn	Brassicaceae
Carrot	2.5–4 cm (1–1.6 inches) in the row, 15 cm (6 inches) between rows	Spring to autumn	Apiaceae
Cauliflower	35–45 cm (14–18 inches)	Spring, autumn	Brassicaceae
Celery	25–30 cm (10–12 inches)	Spring to autumn	Apiaceae
Chard	25–35 cm (10–14 inches)	Spring to autumn	Amaranthaceae
Coriander	10–20 cm (4–8 inches)	Spring, autumn	Apiaceae
Courgette	90 cm (36 inches)	Spring and summer	Cucurbitaceae
Cucumber	35–45 cm (14–18 inches)	Spring and summer	Cucurbitaceae
Eggplants	30–45 cm (12–16 inches)	Spring and summer	Solanaceae
Endive	20–30 cm (8–12 inches)	Autumn to spring	Asteraceae
Fennel	15–30 cm (8–12 inches)	Spring to autumn	Apiaceae
Garlic	10–15 cm (4–6 inches)	Autumn	Liliaceae

Jeruslam artichoke	25–35 cm (10–14 inches)	Autumn to spring	Asteraceae
Kale	30 cm (12 inches)	Spring, autumn	Brassicaceae
Kohlrabi	20 cm (8 inches)	Spring, autumn	Brassicaceae
Kumara	30 cm (12 inches)	Early summer	Convolvulaceae
Leek	10–15 cm (4–6 inches), 30 cm (12 inches) between rows	Spring, autumn	Liliaceae
Lettuce	20–30 cm (8–12 inches)	Spring to autumn	Asteraceae
Melon	30–45 cm (12–18 inches)	Spring and summer	Cucurbitaceae
Miner's Lettuce	2.5–4 cm (1–1.6 inches) in the row, 15 cm (6 inches) between rows	Autumn to spring	Montiaceae
Mustard greens	2.5 cm (1 inch) in the row, 10 cm (4 inches) between rows	Spring to autumn	Brassicaceae
Onion	10–15 cm (4–6 inches)	Winter and spring	Liliaceae
Parsley	10–20 cm (4–8 inches)	Spring to autumn	Apiaceae
Parsnip	5 cm (2 inches) in the row, 15 cm (6 inches) between rows	Spring, autumn	Apiaceae
Pea (climbing)	10 cm (4 inches), one or double row	Autumn to spring	Fabaceae
Pea (dwarf)	10–15 cm (4–6 inches)	Autumn to spring	Fabaceae
Pepper	30–45 cm (12–16 inches)	Spring and summer	Solanaceae
Potato	25–35 cm (10–16 inches)	Spring and summer	Solanaceae
Pumpkin and squash	50–100 cm (20–40 inches)	Spring and summer	Cucurbitaceae
Radish and turnip	2.5 cm (1 inch) in the row, 10 cm (4 inches) between rows	Spring to autumn	Brassicaceae
Rocket	2.5 cm (1 inch) in the row, 10 cm (4 inches) between rows	Spring, autumn	Brassicaceae
Spinach	10–15 cm (4–6 inches)	Spring to autumn	Amaranthaceae
Spring onion	15 cm (6 inches) between clusters of 6	Spring	Liliaceae
Strawberries	25–35 cm (10–14 inches)	Autumn and winter	Rosaceae
Sweet corn	25–30 cm (10–14 inches)	Spring and summer	Poaceae
Tomatillo	50–100 cm (20–40 inches)	Spring and summer	Solanaceae
Tomato	25–50 cm (10–20 inches)	Spring and summer	Solanaceae
Yacón	60–100 cm (24–40 inches)	Autumn to spring	Asteraceae
Watermelon	30–45 cm (12 –18 inches)	Spring and summer	Cucurbitaceae

Right Désirée potatoes.

The Abundant Garden

Chapter 10

Plant health and managing pests and disease

When gardening using a regenerative approach, preventing problems of crop health and pest damage starts at the ecosystem level. Although the vegetable garden is an artificial environment, when you focus on mimicking natural systems you can improve its ecosystem health and cultivate its resilience to pest and disease.

The garden as a healthy ecosystem

It takes time to develop a vegetable garden that sustains a healthy ecosystem, both above and below the soil. As you increase your soil fertility, conditions for growing vegetables will improve over the seasons, and your plants will grow better and provide you with higher yields compared with earlier years.

The Abundant Garden

To create a healthy, nature-inspired ecosystem, create habitats that birds, insects and other small creatures can live and thrive in. By creating an environment thriving with life, the odds are good that when a harmful intruder enters your ecosystem, there will be something there waiting to eat it. A healthy garden needs a small population of pests, otherwise predators we are encouraging won't have anything to eat. We want there to be a dynamic equilibrium, where if a pest increases its numbers, there will be a predator ready to jump up on the opportunity to feed and reduce its numbers.

These habitats take many forms, such as annual or perennial planting, small pools of water or a pile of brush tucked away in the corner. The idea is to create specific niches in and around the garden. Managed meadows can be a fantastic source of food for many beneficial insects and can be mowed in the summer after flowering has ended and then left to regrow with the autumn rains. Try to have some flowering plants year-round, especially in winter when flowers are scarce, as some predators feed on nectar in their adult stage while their young prey on garden pests. Growing cover crops, or leaving a few plants untrimmed to go to seed, can provide a habitat and even a food source for our predator friends to overwinter. Most cover crops, and any vegetable plants from the Asteraceae, Brassicaceae and Amaranthaceae families will do the trick.

Small to medium bushy perennial plants, planted around or in proximity to the vegetable garden, can offer long-term accommodation and a food source for insects and birds. They can be planted individually, in clusters, or small hedgerows to act as a windbreak. Native plants are a good choice as they are naturally part of the ecosystem and require low maintenance.

Your planting can include a variety of sources of food or medicine. A diversified orchard or food forest are great ways to do this. Last century when hedgerows were being cut down in England, the birds left because there was nowhere to nest, and as a result there was a major outbreak of pests. If you create unique habitats beyond your vegetable plants for your friendly predators to live in, they will make your garden their home. They are just waiting for the invitation!

Insect hotels are not necessarily the best solution. Parasites tend to colonise and overtake these permanent structures; in natural settings, the insects would have changed regularly with the seasons.

Below Fennel plants flowering.

Healthy soil ecology

In chapter 2 we discussed how to cultivate a complex biological community in our soils. A healthy, rich and complex biological community in our soil feeds our plants in the best possible way and is the basis for healthy plant growth. Support this rich biological community by providing the soil with diverse organic matter. Inoculating the soil with beneficial microbes, keeping it moist and protecting it by not leaving it exposed are good strategies. When you add high-quality compost to your soil, you are feeding and enhancing your soil community. By regularly providing the soil life with fresh food, you are allowing a more complex web to develop and flourish, thus increasing its ability to keep plants safe from soil pathogens. Weekly or fortnightly foliar sprays of seaweed, molasses, fermented microbial brews, compost tea and fish are all great ways of feeding that community and introducing more beneficial microbes.

Field sanitation

Field sanitation is another way to keep your ecosystem healthy. Although you want to create a complex web of life in your garden, you also want to keep your garden clear from infected plant material.

Clean up any pest-damaged crops and diseased plant residues that you are concerned will spread or stay in your garden. It is better not to compost these plants, as these problems may spread through your garden when you use the compost. To be on the safe side, discard them as green waste so they can be composted in a large facility, where the temperature is controlled for a hot composting process.

As plant lovers, we tend to bring lots of different plant material into our garden. Be careful with plants from another gardener or nursery, as they may bring pests, weeds or diseases. Prevention is much better than cure.

Growing healthy plants

Healthy plants that experience a good life with less stress have a better ability to handle pest and disease pressure. The first line of defence is to take care of your plants' health and to provide them with the conditions for continued growth.

As gardeners who grow plants in natural conditions, there is a lot that is beyond our control. To grow well, plants prefer relatively stable conditions, and can get stressed when the weather fluctuates. Try to grow plants in their optimal season when the weather is considered 'more reliable', and consider using growing covers as extra protection.

Growing successions of the same vegetable that follow each other a few weeks or months apart will also create a more resilient system. Each succession will experience different conditions, and plants will succeed to varying degrees, thereby spreading the risk and providing a more reliable harvest.

Sometimes crops do really well at certain times of the year, and not at others. Consider growing crops only in the seasons that they thrive in your garden. If a crop is repeatedly not doing well in your garden, and you have tried a few varieties without success, we suggest that you just stop growing it.

Grow healthy, resilient plants by:

- growing vigorous vegetable varieties and using fresh seeds in their acceptable seasonal range
- growing transplants with sufficient growing media and keeping them well watered
- hardening off transplants, to prevent a sharp change in conditions before transplanting; transplant seedlings while they are at their peak, so they enjoy uninterrupted growth and avoid transplanting shock
- accommodating the plants' preferences for location, sunlight, fertility, watering, drainage and ventilation; often simply increasing or reducing your watering will resolve disease and pest issues
- foliar-spraying liquid fertilisers and adding additional compost for long-term crops

Below Happy lettuce plants.

- using cloches to create a more suitable growing environment when needed
- following a crop-rotation plan for your main crops.

Disease management

Focusing on plant health is the best thing you can do to prevent fungal, viral and bacterial diseases from affecting your plants, especially when looking at ventilation and watering practices. Increased crop spacing, which improves air circulation, will help plants that are susceptible to fungal disease to grow stronger.

After creating the best possible environment for your plants to thrive, the seed line is the next most important factor in determining a crop's productivity and potential resilience. Choosing disease-resistant varieties makes a huge difference. This is especially true for Cucurbitaceae, which suffer from powdery and downy mildew, and Solanaceae, which can suffer from early and late blight. Additionally, almost all crops have varieties that are better suited to different environments. If a variety is grown in conditions that are very different from what it was bred for, it will not do well.

Over the years, we have trialled hundreds of varieties of plants. Growing two or three lines side by side, we clearly saw that a productive, disease-resistant variety can produce two or three times more yield than a variety not bred with disease-resistance in mind. Our recommendation is to try a few varieties that seem promising, in small numbers, and test for your own conditions.

As with any disease-related problems in the garden, early detection is essential as it allows you time to reduce the damage done and to stop it from spreading. If the crop is towards the end of its life cycle, pull it out of the ground, removing it from the garden's ecosystem completely.

Rust

Rust is a plant disease caused by a fungus from the order Pucciniales. Rust fungi are said to be crop-specific, but as they are airborne, they can travel far and wide. This means that rust can become established in whole regions, and even if you successfully remove

Above Bok choy under Number 8 wire hoops and bird netting.

it from your garden, it can quickly blow in from a neighbouring property. The disease is rust-coloured and is relatively common in garlic, broad beans, snapdragons, wheat, mallows, oats and corn. Affected plants don't die quickly, but their growth will be stunted. Infection is limited to the upper parts of the plant parts, and it doesn't spread to the plant's roots.

Ways to control rust include:

- using rust-resistant varieties
- crop rotation
- raw milk tea foliar sprays
- increased plant spacing to improve air circulation
- early removal of infected leaves from the garden
- early planting of garlic to allow it to grow with a head start and hopefully avoid regional cross-infection
- mulching the bed to keep the soil moisture at consistent levels.
- some growers recommend organic sulphur sprays (we have never tried this)
- some growers also recommend sprays of *Bacillus subtilis* bacteria, which can prevent rust from spreading on to your plant; we have tried this but could not see a significant improvement.

Powdery and downy mildew

Powdery and downy mildew are plant diseases caused by a fungus from the orders Erysiphales and Peronosporaceae, respectively. It is easy to identify powdery mildew as it is highly visible and distinct. It usually starts with white spots that spread from the lower leaves to the top of plants, including their stems. The spots expand and eventually cover the whole plant. In contrast, downy mildew has yellow spots that expand and turn brown.

Downy mildew spreads via spores through the air, and powdery mildew spreads via sucking insects such as aphids.

Preventative methods include:

- growing disease-resistant varieties
- watering by drip irrigation rather than sprinklers or overhead watering

- growing under cover to protect from rain and dew
- increasing ventilation by planting in a location with good airflow and giving each plant enough space
- strict three or four-year crop rotation.

Once the crop is infected, you can:

- remove the infected leaves
- remove the specific succession that is infected; plants are more susceptible when they are older, and at some point, it is best to remove them
- try baking soda sprays, at a rate of 1 teaspoon per litre of water
- try sprays of Neem oil (use restricted in organic agriculture)
- try sprays of *Bacillus subtilis*, which might stop it from spreading on to your plants (it didn't work for us).

Blight

Late blight is caused by a water mould, *Phytophthora infestans*, which harms mainly potatoes and tomatoes. Blight thrives in cooler temperatures and is spread by the wind over long distances. Symptoms include the appearance of dark blotches on the leaf tips and stems, while white mould can appear under the leaves. Late blight doesn't survive long in the soil and needs a host plant from the Solanaceae family to hibernate on.

Early blight is caused by the fungi *Alternaria solani*. The symptoms are brown or black spots in a distinctive 'bullseye' pattern and can also cause stem lesions and fruit rot on tomatoes. It usually occurs on older leaves, and it often causes leaves to become yellow.

Preventative methods include:

- choosing disease-resistant varieties
- crop rotation
- obtaining potato seeds from certified sources
- clearing any infected plant material, including other Solanaceae members
- clearing potential weed hosts such as black nightshade

- planting in free-draining soil with proper air circulation
- mulching to avoid spores from the ground splashing onto the leaves
- watering only from below, as dry leaves do not get infected
- growing under the cover of a tunnel house or field cloches
- staking and pruning tomatoes only when it is dry.

Once the crop is infected, remove any infected leaves or plants. Although copper spray can extend the life of the plants by two to four weeks, it is highly toxic and is not a solution we recommend.

Pest management

Garden pests are any animal that causes damage to your crop. When it comes to pest management, we use an Integrated Pest Management (IPM) approach. This means carefully considering all available pest control techniques and integrating appropriate measures that discourage the development of pest populations. IPM emphasises the growth of a healthy crop with the least possible disruption to ecosystems and encourages natural pest-control mechanisms.

The principles of this system are based on these components:

- acceptable pest levels
- preventative cultural practices
- monitoring
- mechanical controls
- biological controls.

Pest problems will be specific to your location. Here are the most common pests we encounter in Aotearoa New Zealand and how to address them.

Aphids
There are many species of aphids; they are often green but can also be brown, yellow, pink, blue or black. Adults are less than 2.5 mm (0.1 inch) tall, pear-shaped with long antennae. They suck plant

sap, causing damage and injecting viral diseases, and they excrete honeydew, which can support mould growth. Most fully grown plants can handle a small population of aphids without being negatively affected.

There are many ways to control aphids:

- Spraying with soapy water.
- Watering with high water pressure (proven to decrease their load by 70–90 per cent).
- Encouraging natural predators such as ladybirds, parasitic wasps, spiders and lacewings, or introducing them in from suppliers that breed them. To attract and maintain aphid-eating insects, plant companions from the Asteraceae and Apiaceae families, as well as sweet alyssum and clover. Most seasons we buy in a small, inexpensive vial with parasitic wasp eggs to prey on aphids when they get out of balance.
- Handpicking them off.
- Covering crops with tightly woven row covers. This is especially important for seedlings as they are more susceptible to aphid damage.
- Avoiding excessive nitrogen fertilisers.
- Spraying with garlic and pyrethrum or with Neem oil (its use is restricted in organic agriculture).

Above Aphids on lettuce.

Birds

Birds are an essential part of a healthy ecosystem. Although most native birds are very welcome in and around the garden, sparrows, quail and other introduced birds are not. Sparrows were introduced to Aotearoa New Zealand to manage pests but not long after, they were considered a pest in their own right. Sparrows feed on seeds and vegetables. In summer, when they have plenty of food available, they don't trouble us. Unfortunately, in autumn, winter and spring, they scavenge for food in the garden. They will eat almost any type of exposed seed in the ground and will also eat the leaves of most plants.

The first line of defence in controlling sparrows and other birds is using crop covers. To protect crops from these birds, we divide our crops into two groups:

1. For transplants, a simple bird-netting cover is adequate. Bird netting is one of the cheapest options for crop protection. Since wind passes through it without resistance, a simple hoop, ground staples or rocks will be enough to secure it. We started out using only bird netting and soon moved to only using woven meshes. If you are already doing all the extra work to cover your crops, you might as well invest in something that also creates a better growing environment. For winter crops, we make sure there aren't any possible entry points for birds. Even the slightest gap will allow them to go in and decimate a crop. As winter turns to spring, they will be less hungry and will not go to as much effort to get into our crops, and we can afford to leave a few gaps without any crop damage and eventually completely remove the covers.

2. Direct-seeded crops can be protected with bird netting, but we prefer to lay a cover directly on the ground and avoid the extra work of installing hoops if we can get away with it. If you plan to leave the crop under a cover throughout its growing cycle, use hoops from the start. If you only need to protect it while it is young, you can grow the crop under a frost cloth or shade cloth. In most cases you can keep the crop covered until it is 2.5–5 cm (1–2 inches) tall, at which point the birds don't find the leaves as palatable. This strategy is suitable for mustard greens, radishes, beets, spring onion and carrots.

Psyllid

Tomato potato psyllid (TPP), *Bactericera cockerelli*, is a winged insect, yellow in colour, 2–3 mm (0.08–0.12 inches) long, that feeds by sucking on tomato, potato, capsicum, chilli, goji berry, tamarillo, eggplant, convolvulus and kūmara (sweet potato). It causes direct damage when feeding, and indirect damage following its secretion of sugars and by transmitting diseases. On tomatoes, the symptoms are the yellowing and stunting of the growing tip and cupping or curling of the leaves. Flowers may fall off the trusses of infected plants, and the fruit that develops may be small and misshapen.

To control the spread of TPP:

- make sure only to bring in clean plant material
- check for psyllids regularly, so you can intervene straight away
- clear all crops at the end of the season, to deprive it of a place to hibernate over winter; also, clear any other wild Solanaceae around your garden.
- you can buy Tamarixia, a tiny parasitic wasp that feeds on psyllids, and it will make your garden its home. It enjoys flowering buckwheat and alyssum (generalist predators, including some kinds of ladybirds, lacewings and hoverfly larvae, will also feed on psyllids)
- cover plants with a tight mesh row cover to prevent TPP from accessing the crop
- spray plants with food-grade diatomaceous earth, which is a very fine powder made from the bodies of fossilised ocean creatures; the tiny particles kill insects without damaging the plants; mix 0.5 cup diatomaceous earth with 2 cups water and place in a sprayer; use a mask to avoid breathing the powder and spray it early morning or late evening to avoid spraying beneficial insects while they are active.

Rabbits

European cottontail rabbits were introduced as a food source and for sport in the nineteenth century and have become a major pest in Aotearoa New Zealand as they don't have any natural predators. Seven to ten rabbits consume the same amount of grass as an adult sheep, and a female rabbit can produce 45 offspring in a year. They will eat various plants in the garden and can cause substantial damage if they are not controlled. You can usually identify the presence of rabbits by their attempts to dig in the garden in search of food and shelter, combined with a relatively even nibble of plant tops, and of course rabbit droppings are a big clue!

There are two main ways to control rabbits.

1. Fencing is by far the best way to control rabbits. We have read about kilometres-long rabbit-proof fencing, and we have done the same for our extensive garden. So, whatever your garden size, you can too! We used 2.5 cm (1 inch) thick grade galvanised hexagonal mesh and spread that around the garden perimeter. The trick is to lay the mesh in an L-shape. Cottontail rabbits can't jump over 40 cm (16 inches) high, so once they reach the fence line, they will try to burrow underneath. If they can't burrow, they will go away, so 20 cm (8 inches) of fence placed on the ground is plenty. Apart from at the gates, this fence gives us almost total protection from rabbits. To avoid the need to mow the area close to the fence line, which can damage the hexagonal mesh, consider laying the fence on a narrow strip of weedmat.
2. Trapping rabbits is another option, using clover or carrots as bait.

Rats and mice

Rats and mice don't need an introduction. They can quickly become a problem around the garden, as they eat sown seeds, damage root and tuber crops and cause disruption in the compost heaps. They love warm areas like compost heaps when the weather turns colder, and the extra food must also be tempting.

Ways to control rats and mice include:

- laying a galvanised mesh around the base of the compost piles
- setting traps to catch them.

Slugs and snails

Slugs and snails are soft-bodied creatures from the class Gastropoda. There are over 1400 native slugs and snails in Aotearoa New Zealand, but it's the introduced species that do the most damage to vegetables. They eat organic matter, both decomposing matter and live plants. Some gastropods, such as tiger slugs, are omnivorous and will also eat smaller slugs. Slugs and snails can move up to 40 metres (132 feet) a day, and they thrive in damp, humid conditions and dislike dry ground. They

The Abundant Garden

live in the soil, under rocks, in rolled weedmat and on plants.

Controlling slugs and snails is a big problem as they self-regulate their population. They hatch from eggs in high numbers, but most slugs stay in the juvenile state. The slime trails they leave behind them indicate to the juveniles to remain young. But when the number of trails decreases, for example, after we have captured many adults, the juveniles mature and take their place.

Slugs and snails are one of the main pests in the organic garden. Using no-dig systems, and having lots of organic matter, means they are less disturbed and have plenty of available food.

There isn't one sure-fire way to control them but using a combination of strategies and techniques will allow you to work around their destructive behaviour.

- To decrease their potential habitats, mow the grass short around your garden.
- Keep gear off the ground; they love living in moist cloches and weedmats.
- Slugs and snails dislike many materials, such as wood-ash, coffee grounds, eggshells and diatomaceous earth. Spreading these materials around beds and along the paths will make your beds less attractive to them.
- Keeping chickens and ducks around the perimeter of the garden will help decrease their population.
- Beer or yeast and molasses attracts slugs and snails. Create a slug trap by filling a container a few centimetres deep with beer or water mixed with yeast and molasses, and the slugs will climb in and drown. You can buy a designated trap, but any container will do, as long as you keep it covered from the rain.
- Place boards as slug traps and collect them during the day. The slugs shelter under the board in the heat of the day — when you lift up the board there will be lots of slugs under it and on its bottom side. We take them in a small container and feed them to our chickens in their coop.
- Handpicking slugs and snails at night-time over the winter and spring is effective. We prefer to avoid this task, as squashing or poking slugs and snails is not our favourite

Above Garden snails.

Left above Luna intrigued with a caught cotton-tail rabbit.

Left below Cut-up plastic bottles protect carrots from slugs and birds.

activity, but getting rid of a hundred or so big ones in a short time is very satisfying. The chickens appreciate this treat!

- Encourage natural enemies, such as hedgehogs (in Aotearoa New Zealand they are pests but elsewhere they are a gardener's friend), birds, frogs, lizards, ground and rove beetles.

Whitefly

Whiteflies are small, about 1.5 mm (0.06 inch), flying insects that live on the underside of leaves. They prefer warm conditions and can attack a wide range of plants such as beans, cabbages, cucumbers, eggplants, tomatoes and ornamentals. They cause damage by sucking plants, injecting saliva, secreting honeydew that attracts mould, and spreading disease. They are easy to identify, and if you shake your plant, they will scatter and fly away. Ways to control whitefly include:

- encouraging natural predatory insects such as ladybugs and lacewing
- vacuuming them — best done early in the morning with a hand vacuum when they are sluggish
- yellow sticky fly tapes attract and capture them
- introducing the parasitic wasp *Encarsia formosa* for biological control.

White butterfly

White butterfly is a prevalent pest to all brassica crops. It appears in the spring and dies off in the winter. It's the chubby green caterpillars who cause the damage. The adults have cream- to white-coloured wings and are black-bodied. They are 2 cm (0.8 inch) long and have a wingspan of 5 cm (2 inch).

Ways to control white butterfly include the following.

- Covering crops with mesh to prevent them from getting to the plants.
- Removing affected plants.
- Encouraging birds and predatory insects to stick around, as many creatures happily feed on the caterpillars.

Protecting crops from insect damage

Different types of mesh are designed to exclude different-sized pests. Large woven mesh can exclude birds and white butterflies, while tightly woven mesh can also exclude whitefly, leaf miners, tomato/potato psyllid and aphids.

- Catch the butterflies with nets. Harry, our farm partner, gave our daughters butterfly nets and they get paid based on how many butterflies they catch.
- Apparently, white butterflies are territorial, and we have heard of gardeners that swear that by cutting plastic-shaped butterflies and placing them in their garden, the white butterflies left. We've never tried this ourselves.
- A weekly spray of the naturally occurring soil bacterium, *Bacillus thuringiensis kurstaki* (Btk). It is only effective at the caterpillar stage and is supposed to be safe and not affect any other crops.

Below Variety of crop covers.

Chapter II
All about compost

Compost is a product of the recycling of organic materials by microorganisms, which occurs in an aerobic environment. Not all composts are created equal; in this chapter, we explain what makes a high-quality compost, how to make it, and how to use it.

Benefits of compost

There are many benefits of including well-made compost in your garden. While all compost enriches the soil with organic matter, compost made from a wide range of materials allows a broader range of microbes to flourish and creates a more complex biological community. This rich biological community provides better nutrition to your plants, as well as helping to keep soil pathogens in check.

Composting in the backyard makes a lot of sense if you are growing a vegetable garden, as you will be able to use materials from your garden as well as your kitchen waste. By composting your kitchen waste, you are preventing it from going to the landfill where it would release greenhouse gases. It's a win–win situation; you get a rich source of organic matter to enrich your garden, and by embedding carbon into the soil, you are contributing to climate-change mitigation.

Compost fertilises the soil by releasing growth-inducing compounds that encourage plant growth, while improving the health of the soil ecosystem, whereas synthetic fertilisers decrease the soil's fertility and health over time. Compost can overcome pH imbalances, allowing plants access to nutrients that would otherwise be unavailable, as well as reducing the effects of toxins in the soil.

The great thing about incorporating compost into your soil is that no matter what your soil type and conditions, it is always beneficial and will always improve the soil structure. In any soil texture, compost increases the water-holding capacity of the soil, making your soil and plants more drought resistant.

In sandy soils, even a small increase in organic matter will have a big impact. If you are working with sandy soils, incorporating compost helps to increase the soil's ability to hold nutrients, improves its ability to hold water, and feeds the soil's microorganisms.

In clay and silty soils, it takes a significant amount of compost to make a difference. If your soil has a high clay component, it is crucial not to work the soil when conditions are very wet. Clay soils can easily compact and become anaerobic. Many of the beneficial soil microorganisms cannot survive in these conditions. If you have clay soils, incorporating compost helps to prevent the compaction. It provides more air space, increases the soil's ability to drain, increases soil fertility, moderates the soil's tendency to form clods, feeds the soil organisms and improves its workability.

Getting the most from your compost

When preparing beds, spread the compost evenly across the garden bed, and embed it shallowly with the rake into the top few centimetres of the soil. This allows the soil microorganisms full access to the compost and encourages plants to extend long roots across the bed. We tend not to use compost as mulch, because when it is exposed to direct sunlight, it will dry out and oxidise, with only the part touching the soil actually feeding the soil microorganisms. If you use other types of mulch on top of your garden bed, you can spread the compost application before applying the mulch layer and without mixing it in.

The thickness of the layer you spread on the bed depends on how much compost you have available. We usually apply a layer of 1–2 cm (0.4–0.8 inches) at a time, up to 5 cm (2 inches) a year. Applications of this thickness make a big difference, and are plenty, especially if you are applying them more than once in the season. This extra investment results in healthier crops and increased yields, especially as you are establishing your garden. Compost is not a substitute for growing in soil and plants should not be planted in pure compost as a growing medium. Compost is not as balanced for nutrients as soil and should therefore be treated as an amendment rather than a substitute.

As we mention in chapter 2, 'little and often' is a much better approach for compost applications, rather than a one-time application in the spring. Compost has no adverse effects on the soil if it is applied in small amounts. Once applied, it will take one to three weeks before the soil's microorganisms' response to the compost is in full swing. Adding compost in excessive amounts, however, can lead to groundwater contamination just like with any other fertiliser.

Most homemade and purchased composts break down over three to five months from being incorporated into the soil. To provide continuous food to your soil microorganism community and your plants, apply additional compost throughout the season. If you are growing a crop that takes three months to grow, you will benefit from following it with another compost application before introducing the next crop. However, if you are growing two

Left above Compost pile made of various materials, including cover crops. This image was taken at a compost workshop.

Left below Compost pile primarily of woodchips and seaweed.

quick-growing crops one after the other, you don't need to apply compost in between them.

If a crop is in the ground for over three months, you will want to provide it with extra nutrition without interrupting the roots of the growing plants; you can simply spread compost on the ground, in a practice called 'side-dressing'. As these crops are already providing a live mulch over the bed, the compost will mostly be in the shade and will not dry out. It takes one to three weeks for plants to respond to side-dressing, depending on the ground temperature. It's remarkable to see how much it improves the plants' vigour and vibrancy. We generally side-dress a layer of compost on our capsicum, courgettes, eggplants and tomatoes, every 10 weeks or so.

When using homemade compost in the garden, you can use it as is, without sieving it, and removing any large particles to the active compost heap for further decomposition. If you wish, you can attach a 1–2 cm (0.4–0.8 inch) metal mesh onto a wooden frame and pass the compost through it before using it in the garden. We only use a sieve for compost when we are creating a potting mix for plant propagation purposes.

The compost-making process

Compost ingredients

Making your own compost is easy and rewarding. You can use a broad range of materials, depending on what is readily available.

The bulk of the compost heap is made with materials that have a varying ratio of carbon to nitrogen. Additionally, high-quality compost includes materials which are primarily used as mineralising and inoculating amendments. However, there are overlaps between these categories; for example, seaweed is used as a nitrogen-rich, mineral-rich and activating ingredient.

The carbon-rich materials add mass to the heap and are the basis for the organic-matter content, which is the key product of the composting process.

Carbon-rich ingredients include:

- cardboard
- dry leaves (best shredded or mowed over if used in abundance)
- mature cover crops
- mature hay
- mature plant stalks
- nut and seed husks
- sawdust (from untreated wood)
- shredded newspaper and office papers (preferably with low amount of coloured images)
- woodchips.

The nitrogen-rich materials stimulate microbial growth and the decomposition of the carbon-rich materials.

Nitrogen-rich ingredients include:

- food scraps and kitchen waste
- grass clippings (with no seed heads)
- coffee grounds
- fish
- manure
- blood
- pine needles
- seaweed
- weeds (with no viable seeds)
- wool
- young hay or cover crops
- urine (not allowed under organic certification).

Garden residues will have variable ratios of carbon to nitrogen, depending on their maturity. Young plants have a higher nitrogen content, while established plants have a balanced carbon-to-nitrogen content, and dry plants at the end of their life cycle have a higher carbon content.

Composting is a relatively forgiving process, and you don't need to be precise about the exact carbon-to-nitrogen ratio; it can just be used as a guideline. As you build your compost heaps, you will be able to observe how your compost heap 'behaves', and use your observations to fine-tune your future piles.

Compost heaps built with excess carbonaceous materials will take a long time to break down; you can fix this by pouring high-nitrogen liquids over the heap, as long as cold winter temperatures aren't the problem. Compost heaps built with excess nitrogen will smell of ammonia for a few days until the materials stabilise. As you build your pile, pay attention that you create a pile that will encourage aerobic conditions. To facilitate this, avoid compacting layers, and alternate with layers that are made of large particles that have plenty of air gaps.

Mineralising, inoculating and activating amendments to your compost include:

- mature compost, which acts as an inoculant at both the start of the process, and during the curing stage
- garden soil, which acts as an inoculant and also helps retain nutrients that would otherwise be lost to the atmosphere or leached out with water
- wood ash from untreated wood, for increased mineral content; ash must be used very sparingly, no more than a dusting over a few layers because of its strong alkaline pH
- small bones or pre-baked and crushed large bones, for increased mineral content, particularly phosphorus
- comfrey leaves, which contain high amounts of potassium, calcium and phosphorus
- seaweed, for increased mineral content and microbial activity; it is especially prized for its wide range of micronutrients
- rock fertilisers, for increased mineral content; volcanic crush rocks, rock phosphate, lime or any broad-spectrum rock fertiliser that you spread directly into the garden will work even better embedded into your compost heap
- molasses, for increased microbial activity and mineral content
- seawater, diluted at 1:100, for increased mineral content; seawater contains all essential plant nutrients, and is a fantastic source of free, accessible nutrients
- biochar (inoculated or not), for a very long-term carbon source; it is a habitat for beneficial microorganisms.

Materials to avoid in compost used in vegetable gardens include:

- human, cat and dog faeces, as they can harbour harmful pathogens
- large quantities of citrus peels, pine needles, large branches and brush
- municipal green waste, such as curbside lawn clippings
- any material that can cause unhealthy growth or introduce toxins to the compost.

Meat, dairy and oil can be added to the compost pile, but they should be incorporated in small amounts. Embed them with dry carbon-rich organic matter, to eliminate any smells and prevent flies from laying eggs in the meat. It is best to decompose such ingredients in a hot compost pile, as it will decrease the chances of pests accessing the pile.

If weeds have visible seed heads, submerge them in a bucket of water for a few days, which will make the seeds rot and lose the ability to germinate.

Although compost has many benefits, most commercial compost doesn't directly provide many minerals to the soil, as it is mostly composed of waste sources, and hasn't been improved with high-mineral substances. Homemade or artisanal compost, depending on the source materials and the amendments added to it, can also be used to mineralise the soil.

Some amendments can be added directly into your soil, but others are much safer if added to your compost heap. For example, wood ash is too alkaline to lay directly on the ground and can damage biological life. Raw animal manure can harbour pathogens and is not safe to use unless it is aged. Under organic certification, there is a compulsory waiting time of over a hundred days between harvest and the time of manure application. For organic blood and bones fertiliser, the waiting time is six months. Through the composting process, raw materials that could have harmful effects if laid directly on the ground are 'softened', pre-digested and embedded in the compost's organic matter, just the way the microbes and plants like it.

Compost is best when it is made from a diverse range of materials,

The Abundant Garden

as it feeds a broader array of microbes and creates a more complex and robust biological community. As we will explain, good compost that has been left to mature will give you the added benefit of being an inoculant of beneficial microbes into the soil, in addition to being a source of quality organic matter and nutrients.

Hot and cold composting

There are two main approaches to making compost, hot and cold composting. In the cold process, you continuously add materials over a long period. Hot composting is done in batches, by accumulating ingredients and building the compost heap over a short period, ranging from a day to about a week. Each method has its pros and cons, and both can result in a high-quality end product if left to mature.

Hot composting

Once the compost heap is prepared, it will quickly heat up because of the biological activity. Depending on the carbon-to-nitrogen ratio of your ingredients, the temperature range and the duration of it will vary. Compost made with a 30:1 carbon-to-nitrogen ratio, which is the industry standard, will result in a heap that heats up to about 50–55°C (122–131°F) for a week or so. Compost made with ingredients with a higher carbon-to-nitrogen ratio will result in a lower peak temperature, creating a product with more stable organic matter, which will stay in the ground for longer. We tend to alternate between different ratios, to provide the soil microbes with a variety of food sources.

Cold composting

Instead of gathering all the compost materials, in cold composting you add them over time as they become available. You will still need to balance the carbon-to-nitrogen ratio, which is often achieved by covering the nitrogen layers, such as your weeds and kitchen waste, with a carbon-rich layer. Covering kitchen waste and other nitrogen-rich materials with a carbon-rich layer will help eliminate potential disturbing smells and keep flies and other pests from accessing them. It's handy to stockpile carbon-rich materials, and store it next to your compost pile so you have them when needed.

Left Yotam raking compost evenly across the bed.

Cold composting tends to attract more pests, so the heap should be built to block their access. Once the container of your compost heap is full, leave it for a few more months for the top layer to decompose fully. Some structures provide access to the bottom layer so that you can harvest the mature compost from the lowest part of the heap, in a continuous feeding system.

Building the compost heap

1. Build your heap in a well-drained location. If needed, fork the ground to improve drainage and the connection of the heap with the soil's biological community. If building the heap in winter, it is best to place a layer of small branches or large stalks at the bottom of the heap that will allow free drainage.
2. Place your compost heap in the shade or semi-shade, to provide a sheltered environment to prevent it from drying out.
3. Build your compost heap in layers, using materials you have in abundance while aiming for a broad range of materials. Alternate between carbon-rich layers of 5–10 cm (2–4 inches) and nitrogen-rich layers of 10–15 cm (4–6 inches). Building the heap layer by layer makes it easier to integrate the amendments, but it works just as well to mix all the ingredients together before filling them into the heap. When you are adding kitchen waste, make sure it is well covered by other materials. If left exposed, the kitchen waste will attract flies and potentially smell.
4. In most compost heaps, oxygen is the most limiting factor for decomposition. Unfortunately, too many gardeners and compost bin manufacturers don't allow enough room for air to enter the heap, which leads to anaerobic conditions. If ventilation is an issue, insert a 10–15 cm (4–6 inch) long pipe with small holes throughout, at the centre of the heap, to improve aeration in the middle of the heap. Alternatively, while layering the heap, you can place sticks in it, and remove them a week or two later to increase the air penetration into the heap.
5. As you build your heap, you can add a layer of amendments on top of either the carbon or the nitrogen layers.
6. As you build the layers, add water to the heap to keep it

Right Compost heap building
— alternating layers of carbon-
rich materials, nitrogen-rich
materials and amendments.

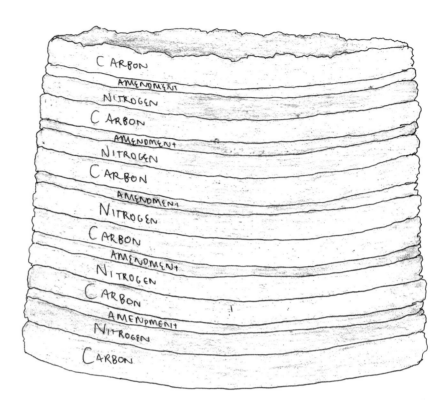

moist, with the same 40–60 per cent moisture content you aim to have in your garden beds. Although you should water your compost heap in the summer, it is harder for water to penetrate throughout the heap, so build it with lots of moisture right from the start.

7. Once you finish making the heap, keep it covered during heavy rains to prevent oversaturation, anaerobic conditions and nutrient leaching. We usually use a tarp to cover our compost heaps over winter.

8. If you are hot-composting, once your heap has cooled down, let the compost cure for another six to ten weeks so that the microbial population can become more complex and spread well throughout the heap. Maximising the compost's abilities to act as a biological inoculant is one of the main advantages of applying compost to your garden, and shouldn't be underestimated.

9. Once the compost has been cured, it should be used within a couple of months or left to dry out and kept under a cover. If the compost is left moist for a long period, it will continue to break down, and will significantly decrease in quantity.

We prefer to keep our compost temperature low, as low-heat composts release less carbon into the atmosphere and conserve more nitrogen, even though they can take six months to a year to fully mature, compared to four to five months for high-temperature compost. Even with their high temperatures, homemade composts are generally not 100 per cent successful at eliminating pathogens or even weed seeds. It's therefore best to keep contaminated materials and plants with viable seeds away from the compost heap. If you want better control over your heap, you can keep a daily track of the compost temperature using a compost thermometer.

When the compost begins to drop in temperature, you can turn it, concentrating on placing the materials that are on the outside of your heap into the centre of the new heap, as they will break down more effectively that way. This will cause the temperature to rise again. Do this several more times until the temperature stops rising. Turning the compost once or twice during the high-temperature stage of the composting process will also help to make the compost more homogenised.

If you are turning the compost heap, take this opportunity to remedy the moisture content of the heap as needed. Add dry matter if the compost is too soggy, or more water if it is too dry.

Compost heaps and bins

We mostly use self-standing compost heaps, but in most home-gardening scenarios a containing structure for making compost is a good idea. Be creative and use whatever is available to construct your composting structure. You can also purchase compost bins and kits.

While the options are endless, make sure that your compost system fits your needs. We recommend choosing a structure that:

- You are fond of using and find attractive, as you will be engaging with it on a regular basis.
- Is physically able to contain the ingredients without

spilling out, while providing ample air circulation.

- Is made of untreated wood. Pallets are generally free and readily available from courier depots, although they don't usually last very long. Hardwood timber can last for over a decade but is harder to source and is generally more expensive.
- Is animal proof. If rats are an occasional problem, placing a fine mesh of 1–2 cm (0.4–0.8 inches) at the bottom of the structure will help prevent them from digging their way in.
- Has a cover which will help control the amount of water your compost heap receives and will prevent oversaturation and leaching of nutrients, as well as drying out of the edges of the heap. The cover can be made of wood, corrugated iron or even a tarp.
- Is of sufficient size. A larger heap will allow for a better ratio of surface area to the inside of the heap and provide better decomposition to most of the materials. Aim for at least a 1 metre (3.3 feet) width, and if you have a relatively large garden, it can be up to 1.5 metres (4.5 feet) wide. The height of the heap can be whatever your structure supports up to 1.5 metres (4.5 feet).
- Has multiple chambers. Most gardeners will find that a two or three compost system structure offers the most flexibility. One bin contains the active heap, one is for curing and one is being used. More than one bin will also allow for easier turning of the heap, and easier fixing of the heap if it needs restructuring.
- Has easy access. Make sure it is easy to take out the ready material. Wooden slats that can be removed or a side of the bin that opens works well.

Having a permanent area for making compost allows compost microorganisms to colonise the area, making the composting process quicker over time, and resulting in a better-quality product.

Install an easy-to-reach hose next to your compost heap, so you can easily water it as well as wash your compost bin.

Place the bin in an area you visit often which is easily accessible from both your kitchen and your garden. Make sure the bin is out of

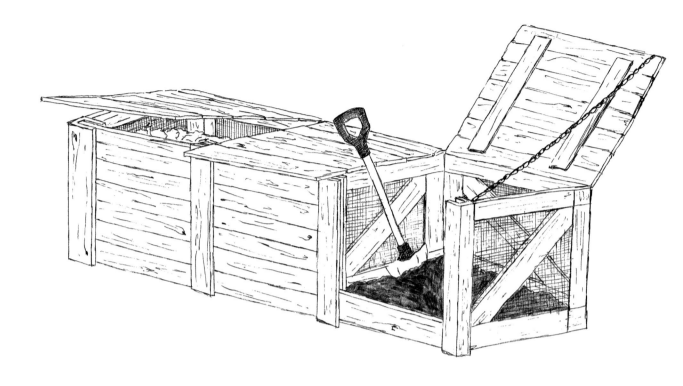

the way of passers-by, and not under any windows; although a well-maintained compost heap will not smell, this is a good precaution in case something goes wrong, for the benefit of your relationship with your neighbours, and to meet some council by-laws.

Keep your compost heap a safe distance from any waterways, to avoid potential contamination. If your water table is very high, consider layering uncharged biochar or sawdust at the base of the heap, and keep the heap covered at all times, to prevent leaching.

To create a stand-alone compost heap (without a surrounding structure), make a slightly tapered shape, wider at the bottom and slightly narrower at the top. These heaps are best made round, and the trick is to make sure that each layer is full. To do this, firmly compact any fluffy layers such as cover crops, especially the outer edges, with shoes or gloved hands. If you leave any gaps, the heap will collapse. Each layer needs to be made from one type of material or materials with similar properties, because different materials will lose volume at different rates, and you want the heap to shrink evenly across to keep it stable.

Other ways to make compost are:
- Vermicomposting. This is the practice of creating a worm farm incorporating the non-invasive red composting worms, *Eisenia fetida*. With the right conditions, they will multiply, and you will have thousands of pets! They require a moist environment of about 80 per cent humidity, and they grow exceptionally well in kitchen waste embedded into strips of wet newspaper or shredded paper. The end product, vermicast, is highly stable and biologically active.
- Tumbling. A tumbler is a rotating bin or barrel that allows you to make compost incredibly quickly. Through frequent rotating, the tumbler disperses microorganisms and increases oxygen, thus accelerating the composting process.
- An old-fashioned way to grow vegetables is to bury kitchen waste in trenches or holes and plant over them. In one of our first gardens, we buried kitchen waste under mulch, but we didn't find this to be a long-term solution. Animals dug up the garden, and the large amount of kitchen waste soon become too much for the small area we had under mulch, and did not decompose fast enough.
- Chickens. Chickens are natural composters, and love to eat most kitchen and garden waste. We continuously dump materials in an area in their yard, which they eat, scratch, turn and poo on. Every few weeks we use a fork to aerate the heap and add various amendments. Every few months we take the compost out of the yard in a heap and spread it around our fruit trees, or we let it cure for several months before using it in the garden, just in case any manure is present.

Buying compost

Depending on your garden size, you might be able to make all of your own compost. Although this is something that many gardeners aspire to, buying in compost and using it lavishly is better than limiting yourself (and your plants) to what you can make on your own. Most of the commercial composts that are available in the market are made from renewable sources and the waste streams of other industries. When buying in compost, there are a few things to keep in mind, so do a bit of research first.

- Purchasing organic compost will be much safer, and will lower the chances of unwanted materials, such as toxic herbicides and fungicides.
- Even with organic compost, there is still a chance of it incorporating unwanted materials. Don't buy it if one of the ingredients is municipal green waste, as it will likely have plants that have been grown in areas that are sprayed with herbicides such as Roundup, which could cause long-term harm to your soil, as well as your health.
- The compost should be clean from weed seeds.
- Although compost made in low temperatures can be of great quality, commercial compost is much safer when it has been kept at high temperatures and frequently turned, to eliminate any pathogens that might be present in the original ingredients.
- The compost should have a pleasant earthy smell, which indicates a decomposition in an aerobic environment. A sour smell indicates anaerobic conditions.
- The compost should be crumbly, relatively even and homogenised, with no visible manure particles.
- The compost should definitely be cold. If it feels warm, or if it warms up after watering, it is not fully mature and should be left to cure for another couple of months. Compost that is applied before it is fully cured can harm plant growth and even prevent germination of some seeds.
- The best compost producers will have batch-tested their compost for nutrients, toxicity and even microbial activity. A good supplier will take pride in the quality of their compost and the practices they use to make it.

Composts vary in price, and although there are bargains out there, you will mostly get what you pay for. If you have a choice, a high-quality compost will more than pay for itself in healthy growth and increased yield. Buying compost in bulk amounts of 0.5–1 cubic metre (cubic yard) or more will lower the price significantly.

Liquid fertilisers

As well as incorporating organic matter in your compost, applying other life-enhancing materials, such as molasses, fish and seaweed fertilisers, will help diversify and feed the microbial community.

Liquid fertilisers offer ample available nutrition to plants, but they don't last for long. It is best to use them often, and while your plants wouldn't say no to a daily spray, once a week or once a fortnight is plenty. For the best results, we alternate between several types of sprays. Having a dedicated sprayer for this purpose and keeping it and the fertilisers close to the garden will make it easier for you to keep up with this practice.

Using a sprayer allows you to spread small quantities of liquid fertiliser over the leaves and soil. It's best to dilute liquid fertilisers with water, in ratios from 20:1 to 100:1. Using a watering can, you can either spread the liquid feed lightly, in similar dilution rates to using a sprayer, or use it to drench your soil at a higher concentration (as much as 10:1) to penetrate the root zone.

Liquid feed applied to a plant's leaves has an immediate effect that plants respond to promptly. A root drench will take a week or two to have an effect, but it will be longer-lasting. A combination of the two is ideal for struggling plants and highly demanding crops. When preparing transplants for planting, soak the whole plant in a weak liquid fertiliser solution to achieve both immediate and longer-lasting effects.

All sprays are best sprayed on overcast days or in the evening, as direct light will harm the microbes. In warmer weather (from spring to autumn), the microbial application will be better able to survive than applying it in cold weather.

Compost tea

Using well-made and fully cured compost to create a liquid fertiliser is a fantastic way to feed your plants. The liquid compost will help spread and inoculate plants and soil with beneficial microorganisms as well as available nutrients.

To make compost tea, place some compost in a mesh or woven sack to contain it, and dunk it in a bucket of water for a few minutes to an hour or so, occasionally stirring it to introduce oxygen. If you have a fish-tank air pump, you can use that to introduce oxygen and keep the bag of compost in the water for longer. To improve the effect of the compost tea, add a bit of molasses so the microbes will have immediate food to feast on.

If you are passing the compost tea through a sprayer, use a fine screen to remove any small particles that might block the spraying nozzle.

Seaweed

Whether you gather it from a pollution-free beach, or buy it in a liquid form, granules or powder, seaweed is a powerful ally. It helps to bind soil particles together to form aggregates, and it contains all the trace elements plants need, as well as growth hormones and amino acids. Washed-up seaweed is one of the most sustainable fertilisers for the garden and therefore we use it often. We compost the seaweed as well as make liquid fertilisers by soaking it in water for a few months. Diluted 1:100, we aim to spray our plants and soil at least once a month.

Seaweed also helps plants develop internal resistance to cold, and is very beneficial in the autumn and winter for vegetables, flowers and trees.

Fish

Homemade or bought fish fertilisers are very potent, as their smell indicates! Fish fertilisers contain a broad range of minerals and trace elements, as well as nitrogen and growth hormones. Because excessive nitrogen can compromise plant health (and because of the strong smell), we use fish liquid feed only occasionally. We usually save it for when we see plants that are struggling or not growing as fast as we expected.

Seawater

There are over 40 minerals found in seawater, including chloride ($Cl-$), sodium ($Na+$), sulphate ($SO_4 2-$), magnesium ($Mg 2+$), calcium ($Ca 2+$), and potassium ($K+$). Clean ocean water when very diluted (about 1:200) is good for mineralising soil.

Below Washed-up seaweed.

The Abundant Garden

Liquid mineral fertilisers

Many of the suggested inputs we mention can be bought or made into liquid form. The key principle is that solid fertilisers have a longer-lasting effect on the soil but take a while to become available to plants. Liquid feeds, on the other hand, are immediately available to the plants, but are not long-lasting.

Compost and solid fertilisers are the basis of soil and plant nutrition, and the liquid foliar feeds are the icing on the cake. Compost and solid fertilisers are best incorporated between crops, whereas liquid feeds are better sprayed during the growing season. In saying that, with some long-term heavy feeding crops, we would apply a second dose of compost and fertilisers mid-season as side-dressing — explained earlier in this chapter — to provide them with an extra boost.

Chapter 12
Growing microgreens

We love growing these quick-growing, seedling-sized plants. Microgreens are sown at an incredibly high density, which provides an abundant harvest from a small space. You can grow them in any size container, and they are easy to grow year-round on a sunny kitchen bench or in a small outdoor structure.

Microgreens are very young plants harvested after the sprout stage and before the baby-leaf stage. They are mostly grown to the cotyledon stage (the first set of leaves), before the true leaves appear, although some varieties can be grown to have one or two sets of true leaves.

Microgreens are versatile in the kitchen and can dress up almost any dish, sweet or savoury. We eat our microgreens as a standalone mixed salad or enjoy eating varieties on their own to celebrate their unique flavour, such as sunflower microgreens. We love eating microgreens abundantly because they are tasty, delicate and beautiful, and are packed with nutrition. There is a growing body of scientific evidence about their value as a nutrient-dense food and the variety of ways they can be used to support people's health.

For example, according to research that tested 10 microgreen varieties, all varieties were 2–3.5 times more nutrient-dense than spinach. Radish was the most nutrient-dense variety, followed by basil. (Ghoora, Babu & Srividya, 2020, *Journal of Food Composition and Analysis*). Another research project found that the vitamin C level of red cabbage microgreens was six times higher than mature red cabbage and that microgreens in general contained far more vitamins and carotenoids than mature plants of the same varieties. (Xiao et al., 2012, *Journal of Agricultural and Food Chemistry*).

Containers

Microgreens grow very rapidly, and can be grown in shallow trays, punnets or any other clean container. If repurposing other containers, make sure they have drainage holes drilled in them. We prefer to use food-grade plastic trays that have flat bottoms. When we stack the trays on top of each other, the flat bottoms provide even pressure on the trays below, resulting in even growth. (If you are not planning to stack your trays, flat-bottomed containers are not essential.) Microgreens can also be sown directly in the ground, as they grow faster than most weeds. Growing them in raised beds will make them easier to harvest.

The container's depth and how much growing media it contains will determine how often you will need to water your trays. Deeper trays require less frequent watering because they offer more room for the potting mix or other growing media to store water. Seedling or punnet trays about 5 cm (2 inches) deep work well in a home setting. We prefer to use shallow containers

Above Clockwise from top left: pea shoots, purple radish, basil, cress, purple basil, rocket, amaranth. Middle: red cabbage.

Page 258 Yotam harvesting pea shoots in the microgreens tunnelhouse.

Page 259 'Fiji feathers' — pea shoot microgreens.

The Abundant Garden

— about 2.5 cm (1 inch) deep — because we like to stack them and are happy to water daily. When the plants are sown at a high density and grow to 10 cm (4 inches) tall, they consume a lot of water on a sunny day.

Our trays are all the same size, which simplifies the sowing process. If you use a few different types of containers, designate one of them as your 'standard' size, and measure the other containers against it.

Location

You can grow your microgreens on a sunny kitchen bench or outdoors. Microgreens are not fussy, and will happily grow in almost any structure you provide for them, as long as they are protected from heavy rain and strong winds. If you are growing them outside, place them under the eaves on the sunny side of your house, where you will have easy access and be reminded to visit regularly. If you don't have problems with birds eating your microgreens, you could get away with placing your trays out in the open.

Microgreens can also be grown alongside your seedlings for transplanting. They grow well on shelves, which helps to maximise the floor space in your growing area. If you do use shelves for growing, place any seedlings you grow for transplanting on the top shelf, and the microgreens on the lower shelves as they don't need as much direct sunlight. We place sheets of Corflute on the top shelves to prevent water droplets from damaging the trays below.

We currently grow our microgreens on shelves in a small tunnel house close to the house. In the past, we have simply grown microgreens on a bench outside, with hoops and a mesh cover in summer, and replaced the mesh with a plastic film cover in winter.

Left Yotam carrying a stack of seeded microgreen trays.

Light

Once they have germinated, microgreens will benefit from being in a sunny spot, with four hours or more of direct sunlight each day. Many microgreens can grow with even lower light conditions, especially peas, which can grow with 100 per cent indirect light. Although you can successfully grow microgreens under artificial lights, we much prefer growing them outdoors under natural light.

If you want your microgreens to grow taller, you can deprive them of light for the first few days after germination. You can easily do this by placing another container of the same size upside down on top of the tray you are growing. This will cause the microgreens to grow leggy and yellow, but once you lift the cover, they will fully colour within two or three days. We like using this technique for growing long-stemmed sunflower shoots, which are a delicacy.

Ventilation

As microgreens are sown very densely, they are particularly susceptible to fungal diseases. The better the airflow, the healthier and stronger your plants will be. If you are growing them inside a structure, having mesh sides will usually be all you need, and there is no need to add fans. It is best to keep trays raised off the ground to improve the airflow around the base of the trays.

Temperature

Each plant variety has a preferred temperature range in which it thrives. Some plants grow better in cooler temperatures (such as radish, cabbage and peas), while others prefer warmer temperatures (such as sunflower, basil and amaranth). If growing outdoors, try to grow different plants in their preferred season. When growing indoors, you can usually grow warmth-loving plants out of season, as long as they get adequate heat and light.

Right Harvesting microgreen trays — peas, radish and red cabbage.

Growing media

Growing media is the substance that a plant grows in, and includes soil, compost, seed-raising mix, potting mix and so on. Microgreens can grow in any media that is suitable for growing transplants. While we use an organic potting mix, certain composts can also be used as a 100 per cent growing media for microgreens. If you are using compost, make sure it is certified organic and fully cured, as it can be a health risk if there are traces of manure still present. If the compost heats up, or smells of manure, wait another few months before using it. If your soil is sandy loam, you could use it as the primary ingredient in your growing media, mixed with compost. Try using your soil mixed with various percentages of compost, to see which results in the best growth, and compare it to microgreens grown in organic potting mix.

If you are experimenting with creating your own media, make sure that it:

- is free-draining for optimal root growth and to prevent rot
- holds moisture so that microgreens won't dry out quickly
- has particle sizes up to 1.5 cm (0.6 inches) for easy rooting (use a sieve to break or filter large particles)
- is free of weed seeds
- holds enough nutrients so that plant growth is optimised.

To save on potting mix, we recycle our 'used' potting mix and use it as the basis of any new trays, by emptying the trays into a dedicated bin to decompose for two to three months. Once fully decomposed, we use the old potting mix as the bottom 75 per cent or so of the new trays, compact that layer a bit to keep it even and then top the tray up with a layer of new potting mix. We find that the layer of new material significantly helps the plants' growth. If you are making your own mix, you can also recycle it in this way

After filling the tray, lightly compact it, so the seeds that you scatter will all be on the same level and will have good contact with the growing media.

Seeds

You can buy specific microgreen seeds from most seed companies, and baby leaf varieties are also a good choice. While most vegetable varieties will be suitable for eating as microgreens, some taste better than others. Although the seeds are not eaten directly as with sprouts, it is still best to use organic seeds. It is important to use seeds with a high germination rate, as otherwise they will rot in the trays. Seeds should also be clean from debris, which can cause mould to proliferate.

When you first try a microgreen variety, order a small packet of seeds. Once you have found which varieties you like and can grow well, consider buying bulk packets to reduce the cost. Unlike other vegetables, microgreens are sown in such high densities that you will use up your seed supply very quickly, and the price per weight reduces dramatically when you buy in bulk.

Seeding

When sowing microgreens into trays, aim to get the highest yield per tray. This helps to make the most of the time and resources you will put into growing them. The optimal sowing rate of each variety changes with the seasons, especially when growing in natural light and unheated environments. You will need to be alert to what changes are needed and when, which you can assess by closely observing the growth and adjusting the sowing rates accordingly.

Measure the number of seeds per tray by using a small measuring cup or a set of measuring spoons. For larger seeds, such as sunflowers, peas and buckwheat, a larger measuring cup will do the trick.

Most seeds can be directly scattered onto the tray, from the measuring cup or your hand, based on the right seeding density for the size of the tray and the plant variety. Scatter the seeds as evenly as you can across the container, by shaking your hand gently, making sure to cover the edges as well as the centre. It takes a bit of practice, but after a few sowings you will become proficient with this technique.

You can grow different microgreen varieties in separate containers, grow two or three varieties side by side in a tray, or blend varieties that have a similar number of days to maturity.

Cover and stacking

After you scatter the seeds onto your tray, water them and keep them in the dark to germinate. You can stack the trays on top of each other, to provide light compaction, and to allow the seeds to germinate in the dark in moist conditions. If you leave the trays unstacked, you will need to find an alternative way to keep the seeds moist while they germinate. You could use an upside-down container of the same size, or any larger-sized light-proof lid. Another method is to add a thin layer of growing media over the broadcasted seeds so the seeds are not visible, using a fine soil sieve.

With most seed varieties, the best time to unstack the trays is when the plants have not only sent roots but also have a growing tip of 0.5–1 cm (0.2–0.4 inches). By this stage, the plants should be well rooted, so no plant should stick to the bottom of the tray above when you unstack the trays. If you cover the seeds with growing media, they will pop out of the soil by themselves. If some growing media sticks to the seedlings, you can gently scrape it off with your hand or a fine mist spray.

Watering

The easiest way to water your microgreens is by hand-watering them with a gentle spray from a spray nozzle. You could also use a watering can, a sprayer, or a regular water bottle if you are just growing a few punnets. Be careful not to change the seeds' distribution over the tray when watering from above.

Bottom-watering is an alternative watering system to watering from above. In this method, you fit your microgreens tray inside another tray without holes and fill the bottom tray with water. You will need extra space for this and a level bench to use this method. Through capillary action, water moves up into the top container

Soaking seeds

Some seeds will benefit from soaking in water for six to eight hours before sowing, particularly larger seeds such as sunflower and pea. Soaking will help to break the seeds from dormancy, resulting in quicker and more even germination. The disadvantage to soaking seeds is that smaller seeds will be much more challenging to handle and spread evenly onto the tray when wet. To alleviate this, we strain soaked seeds with a sieve and let them dry for about half an hour before sowing.

If you encounter mould on your trays, you can add a little vinegar or another type of organic sanitiser such as hydrogen peroxide or ANK analyte while soaking the seeds, to eliminate any seed-borne fungal disease.

and keeps the soil moist. Bottom-watering reduces watering time and is effective at keeping leaves dry.

A more advanced option is to use a bottom-watering bench, which is a table with sides and a liner that can hold water for a large number of trays. This set-up might be excessive if you are only growing microgreens, but it can also be used to grow transplants. You can even set up a pump that automatically fills and drains the table. Ensure that water doesn't stay in the tray for more than a few hours, in case conditions at the bottom of the container turn anaerobic.

How much water is needed is an ever-changing balancing act between several factors.

- The size of the microgreens. Larger microgreens transpire more and need more water. However when the microgreens are small, the potting soil is exposed and can dry out more easily on sunny days.
- Strong winds draw away moisture and dry the soil.
- Sun and heat cause water to be lost to transpiration and evaporation.

Aim to water so the leaves dry out as quickly as possible while the soil stays moist for as long as possible. As the leaves are at an unusually high density, high levels of humidity increase the chance for rot and mould. While you should always water plants if they are wilting and thirsty for water (and ideally before that), it is best to water only when you know that the leaves will dry out before it gets dark. If it is too late in the day, only water if the leaves have wilted.

If you know you are going to be away during the day, and that the trays will need to be watered before you return, definitely water in the morning before you leave the house. Otherwise, it is best to water after the sun is high enough in the sky to dry the leaves and warm the soil to balance the cooling effect of the watering.

If your trays become very dry, they will need consecutive watering in two or three short intervals. The first watering helps the soil to 'open up' and receive water instead of resisting it. Once the water from the first round has percolated in, the second and third rounds guarantee the trays are thoroughly moist all the way through. This is also an excellent way to water in the middle of most hot summer days, as any excess water will just drain away. It is best not to water at all when the soil in the tray is moist. In winter, this can mean as little as one watering every other day.

Harvesting and cleaning

Microgreens can either be harvested at the cotyledon stage, before the true leaves appear, or with several sets of true leaves. It depends on your personal preference and which plants you are growing. You can choose to only harvest part of your tray and leave the rest for another time. As long as the plants are not past their peak, you can keep enjoying the freshest microgreens over a few days.

Mornings are the best times for harvesting microgreens. They are at their peak at this time of day, and become less crisp when they heat up later in the day.

Cut the microgreens with a sharp knife a few millimetres above the potting mix. You can also use kitchen scissors to harvest small amounts if you prefer. Gently hold the microgreens while cutting them, giving a little tug to make them taut while being careful not to uproot them.

If your microgreens are clean and you have harvested them carefully, you can eat them straight from the tray without washing them, especially if they were grown indoors. We wash our microgreens in a tub of water, to make sure they are completely clean before we use them. If you are not planning to use your microgreens shortly after washing them, use a salad spinner to dry them before storing in the fridge. Once harvested, microgreens can be kept in the fridge for about 10 days.

Most microgreens don't regrow after you have cut them. The only exceptions we know of are peas and sorrel, which can grow a second flush. Once harvested, you can recycle and reuse the potting mix by composting it. After harvesting, let the potting mix and roots decompose for two to three months until the roots decompose entirely. We use this recycled potting mix to grow more microgreens as explained earlier and for compost for the

Below Harvested peashoot trays on their way to be composted for reuse.

The Abundant Garden

garden. Alternatively, you can lay the tray upside down with the roots facing up directly on top of your garden bed or around your fruit trees as compost.

Which microgreens should you grow?

Almost all vegetables and herbs can be grown and eaten as microgreens, even cucumbers, borage and lettuce. Despite the endless possibilities, some varieties are better to grow than others. These are the tastier, cheaper and quicker-growing varieties that lend themselves to high-seeding density and offer high yields per tray in return.

The most prolific microgreens to grow are *radish, sunflowers and peas*. They grow to be harvest-ready in seven to fourteen days depending on the season, and they yield 500 g to 1 kg (1.1 to 2.2 pounds) in our 46 x 35 cm (18.4 x 14 inch) trays.

Amaranth

Amaranth, especially the magenta-coloured variety called 'Red Garnet', is another beautiful and nourishing microgreen. Amaranths, with their tiny seeds, grow much better in warmer weather and take about three weeks to reach a harvestable stage. Their yield is generally low, and their taste is average, but their stunning colours make them worthwhile in small amounts.

Basil

We love growing both the green and purple varieties of this aromatic herb, which can provide a substantial yield. Basil microgreens like to grow in warm weather, and do best in a rich potting mix with lots of water. Once the seeds get wet, they become mucilaginous and therefore are best broadcasted dry, without soaking. The seeds tend to stick to the tray above them, so it's better not to unstack them until the shoots come up. They can take two to three weeks to reach a harvestable stage and can be enjoyed with their true leaves. The purple varieties tend to be more cold-tolerant and can be grown around the shoulders of the season.

The Abundant Garden

Beet

Beets are a more challenging microgreen to grow, as their germination is not consistent. Soaking them and then sieving the seeds so they dry a little for easier handling seems to help with germination. After broadcasting the seeds, cover the seeds with the growing media, and lightly compact the layer, as this helps the greens to emerge without their seed hulls. Beets can be grown year-round, but prefer to grow in cool environments. There are stunning colours of beets available, including red, purple and yellow. Let them grow a set of true leaves, which increases their weight. They take two to three weeks to reach a harvestable size and offer a relatively lower yield.

Brassicas

Broccoli, cabbage, cress, kale, kohlrabi, mizuna, pak choi, rape and rocket all make terrific microgreens, which can be enjoyed past the cotyledon stage, and vary in shape, colour and taste. From the milder kohlrabi and mizuna to the spicy cress and rocket, these microgreens can all grow year-round, with their spicy taste intensifying in summer. Seeds vary in size, but they are all relatively small compared to radish. Most of these seeds yield well, but will generally take 10 to 18 days to reach a good weight. These microgreens are generally reliable, though a good seed source makes a huge difference. The seeds don't need soaking or sanitising.

Buckwheat

Buckwheat microgreens can grow year-round but prefer cooler environments. They offer a mild flavour with a melting texture and are very nice in salads. The seeds benefit from soaking and can be easily handled when wet. Buckwheat microgreens are relatively quick to grow, and provide a mid-range yield. They are best eaten at the cotyledon stage.

Pea

Pea shoots are sweet, crunchy and not at all spicy. They are very versatile and are great in salads, as well as added to cooked dishes such as stir-fries. Peas are prolific and come in many varieties.

Left Beet microgreens.

Our favourite pea variety is 'Fiji Feathers'.

Peas are quick to reach a harvestable size, and they offer the best return when they are about 10–12.5 cm (4–5 inches) long, before they become stringy. They can grow year-round, but prefer cooler environments, and can grow without any direct light. The seeds benefit from soaking and they can be harvested a second time, though the second harvest will often be of lesser quality and offer lower yields.

Radish

Radish microgreens come in various colours, and we like mixing purple, green and pink varieties together. Harvest the radish at the cotyledon stage, as the true leaves are unpleasant to eat, especially in non-microgreen varieties. Radish microgreens are considered one of the most nutrient-dense microgreens, which makes it worth eating them on a daily basis. Radish microgreens can be grown year-round, and are very prolific. With their relatively large brassica seeds, they grow extremely quickly, and are ready within seven days in summer and about two weeks in winter.

If you'd like to grow the green, pink and purple microgreens in the same tray, you will need to soak the pink and purple radish seeds for four to eight hours before scattering them in a tray with the dry green seeds. If you don't soak the seeds, the green radish microgreens will grow faster than the pink and purple varieties, hindering their growth.

Sunflower

Sunflowers are an incredible microgreen, with a nutty, sweet taste, mild pungency and a crunchy texture. They are also highly nutritional, packed with vitamins and minerals such as zinc, potassium, magnesium, iron and selenium. Sunflowers are very prolific and fast-growing, offering high yields. They should be eaten while at the cotyledon stage, as their true leaves have an irritating texture.

Sunflowers grow over the warmer part of the year, and to grow them well, there are a few things that make a big difference. Firstly, soak the seeds with a little vinegar or other sanitiser. Once seeds are sown, place a heavy weight on their tray, such as a brick,

Right Radish microgreens.

Growing microgreens

Above 'Red Garnet' amaranth microgreens.

Left Rainbow microgreens mix.

The Abundant Garden

to help them root and grow well. Once the weight is lifted and the trays are unstacked, they will benefit from light deprivation for a few days, to help them develop a long stem. We usually place the same-sized tray upside down on top and leave it covering the tray until the shoots are over 5 cm (2 inches) tall.

Sunflower seed hulls sometimes stick to the leaves, but often they will fall off if the plants are allowed to grow a bit longer. If the seed hulls are persistent, you can water the plants to soften the hulls and then brush your hand on the tops of the plants to shake them off.

Other herbs

Other herbs that we like growing as microgreens include coriander, chervil, dill and sorrel. All of these can be grown year-round, though they prefer cooler environments. They take longer to grow, usually around three weeks, and as their yield is relatively low, we only grow them in small amounts for their unique flavours.

Microgreens growing information

	Days from seed to harvest	Yield	Growing season
Radish	7–14	Very high	Year-round
Sunflower	7–10	Very high	Summer
Pea	7–14	Very high	Year-round
Rocket, cress	10–14	Medium	Year-round
Broccoli, cabbage, kale, kohlrabi, mizuna, pak choi, rape	14–21	High	Year-round
Basil	14–21	Medium	Summer
Amaranth	14–21	Low	Summer
Beets	18–24	Low	Year-round
Buckwheat	10–14	High	Year-round
Herbs	17–28	Low to medium	Year-round

Microgreens sowing sheet

	Summer sowing rate for a 33 x 28 cm (13 x 11 inch) container	Winter sowing rate for a 33 x 28 cm (13 x 11 inch) container
Radish	25 ml (5 tsp)	30 ml (6 tsp)
Sunflower	200 ml (0.85 cups)	-
Pea	300 ml (1.25 cups)	270 ml (1.1 cups)
Rocket, cress	6 ml (1.2 tsp)	10 ml (2 tsp)
Broccoli, cabbage, kale, kohlrabi, mizuna, pak choi, rape	10 ml (2 tsp)	15 ml (3 tsp)
Basil	12 ml (2.5 tsp)	-
Amaranth	5 ml (1 tsp)	
Beet	20 ml (4 tsp)	25 ml (5 tsp)
Buckwheat	25 ml (5 tsp)	35 ml (7 tsp)
Chervil, dill	12 ml (2.5 tsp)	20 ml (4 tsp)
Coriander	25 ml (5 tsp)	30 ml (6 tsp)
Sorrel	5 ml (1 tsp)	8 ml (1.5 tsp)

The Abundant Garden

Please use this table as a rough guide and a starting point for your own experiments. Seed sizes and therefore sowing rates can change between varieties, and even batches of the same variety from the same supplier can have variations. The general rule for sowing density is: the smaller the seed, the smaller the sowing rate.

In this table, we used a standard-size seedling/microgreens tray.

Experiments with microgreens

When growing microgreens, there are many parallels to growing vegetables in the garden. Growing microgreens could be viewed as having a 'micro garden'. As you learn to grow microgreens well, you will improve your observation skills, which will in turn help you develop your vegetable gardening skills.

Some batches of microgreens will inevitably do better than others. As you try to figure out what factors have affected their growth and yield, it is helpful to be systematic with your experiments. Although single trays that have been managed differently can offer valuable insights, when you undertake an experiment, you will get more consistent results by comparing several trays with only one variable (a factor that changes) between the groups. Repeating the experiment more than once will give you further confidence in your conclusion.

As microgreens are grown in a relatively delicate system, many factors affect their health, so it is not always straightforward to figure out why growth has been affected. Once you have repeatedly observed a better way to grow and manage your microgreens, you should make these changes 'official' and implement them going forward.

Yield is lower than expected

Cause of the problem	Possible solution
Seed density is too low	Experiment with higher seeding densities. If plants grow small and stocky, that is an indication of a low seeding density.
Growing media is stale or not adequate for growing microgreens	Experiment with using different recipes when making your own growing media, or try a different supplier of potting mix. Some varieties (such as radish) can grow in almost any media, while most other plants need better conditions.
The temperature range is not optimal	If conditions are too hot or too cold for a specific crop, they will not germinate or grow well. Move trays to a warmer or cooler location, or take a break from growing that variety until the season changes.
Not enough light deprivation (sunflowers)	Try keeping trays stacked longer or cover with another tray for a few more days.

Uneven or low germination rate

Cause of the problem	Possible solution
Growing media is too dry during germination	Water the trays before or after seeding. If trays are not stacked, they will need frequent watering.
The trays have been unstacked too early and some seeds have dried out	Unstack the trays only after you notice about 1 cm of growth on the plants.
There isn't good contact between seed and the growing media	Compact the growing media before or after sowing.
The temperature range is not optimal	If conditions are too hot or too cold for a specific crop, they will not germinate or grow well. Move trays to a warmer or cooler location, or take a break from growing that variety until the season changes. In the summer, you can add a shade cloth over your growing area, which will provide a cooler environment for your plants.
Seeds are not microgreens or high-quality varieties	Soak seeds for four to eight hours before sowing to improve germination. Try a different seed source.
The seeds are too old	Buy new seeds.
Birds or rodents are eating your seeds	Add extra protection to your growing area, perhaps with hoops or a wooden structure with a mesh.

Uneven growth

Cause of the problem	Possible solution
Growing media is too dry during the growing stage	This usually occurs over half the tray or along the edges and dry areas can be seen on adjacent trays. Water the trays more evenly and for longer.
The bench is not level.	This can cause uneven pressure on the stacked trays, causing some areas of the tray to grow better or faster. Water can also run off too quickly from the higher part of the tray, leaving it dry. Level the bench.

Mould or rot

Cause of the problem	Possible solution
Overwatering	Prevent overwatering by only watering when the trays are starting to dry out, but before they start to wilt. Only water in the middle of the day or when the leaves have time to dry out.
Seed density is too high.	Lower the seeding rate and experiment to find the optimal seeding rate.
Not enough light	Move to a sunnier location.
Inadequate ventilation	Change location or create better ventilation by adding vents or a fan.
Trays stacked for too long or too high	Try unstacking earlier and make a smaller stack.
Seed-borne mould	Sanitise seeds when soaking, and spray with diluted sanitiser when unstacking trays. This is a common issue with sunflower and pea microgreens.
Low quality or old seed	Order new seed or change variety.

Other problems

Problem	Possible solution
Black spots on leaves	This is common in winter and spring and is caused by small fly bites. Hang sticky fly tapes above the trays to catch the flies.
Seeds stick on leaves	Let plants grow for longer. Water the plants with more pressure before harvesting.
Rodent or bird damage	Add extra protection to your growing area, perhaps with hoops or a wooden structure with mesh. We have lots of bird pressure in our garden and have to protect our microgreens this way.

Chapter 13
Saving seeds

Saving seeds from the plants you grow is very satisfying. It gives you a deeper connection to your plants' full life cycle. Plants from the Asteraceae, Brassicaceae and Amaranthaceae families are magnificent to look at when they go to seed.

Seeds from some plants such as tomato and squash can be saved very easily. When you save your own seeds, you complete your part of the ancient deal, the 'pact' that gardeners throughout time have made with plants: 'I will grow you and help you multiply, and you will feed me.'

There are many benefits to saving the seeds of your favourite vegetables. When done well, saving seeds can help you acclimatise your plants to better suit your particular growing conditions, which, in turn, will reward you with healthier plants and higher yields. You can also save the seeds of any surplus plants or plants you didn't get to harvest before they started bolting. Although you won't be saving them to preserve the seed line, you can still grow them to eat, save a bit of money and enjoy the process.

Saving your own seeds well will help make sure the varieties you love will continue to be available, even if the place you bought the seeds from no longer stocks them. Many of today's popular seed varieties are the work of home gardeners, who for generations have saved seeds of their favourite varieties. Every time you save your own seeds, you are effectively breeding your plants. There are a few things to consider when saving seeds with this goal in mind, as the seed lines need to stay pure and vigorous.

When you save seeds, you will usually harvest far more seeds than you can use. This is an excellent opportunity to share your seeds with others, and swap seeds with your neighbours and other gardeners in your community. You can collaborate with friends, with each of you saving seeds from different vegetables and sharing the seeds between you. Look out for local seed-swap groups and community seed banks, as these are great initiatives developed to assist and support gardeners to save and share seeds, and preserve treasured seed varieties that are not commercially viable. We love taking part in local swaps, as it is an excellent opportunity to connect with like-minded gardeners, share the seeds of our favourite varieties, and receive exciting seeds as well.

Seed-saving basics

Open pollinated and hybrid varieties

The best vegetable seed lines to save from your garden are open-pollinated varieties. This means that the parents of the plants you are saving seeds from are the same variety, and that their offspring are likely to have very similar properties to their parents.

Unlike genetically modified seeds, hybrid varieties are relatively harmless and are a result of crossing parents from two or more varieties. Although their direct offspring, referred to as F1, have specific desirable characteristics, their grandchildren's generations (F2) and beyond will most likely be very different and vary widely, and therefore won't provide reliable results. There are good reasons to use hybrid seeds in the garden; often hybrid seed varieties will be more vigorous, disease-resistant and higher-yielding than open-pollinated varieties. Most of the worldwide multi-billion

The Abundant Garden

dollar commercial seed growing industry is focused on improving hybrid varieties, as these seeds can be sold for a higher price point, and will encourage customers to keep on coming back, instead of saving seeds from the plants. The disadvantage of growing hybrid seed varieties is that they are not always chosen or bred for the best flavour and that considerations like shelf life and uniformity take precedence.

Some hybrids are more simple crosses than others, with relatively small variations. If you are happy to experiment, you might find that you can easily save many hybrid lines, especially baby leafy greens, root vegetables and herbs, with good results. In the Cucurbitaceae and Solanaceae families, the crosses tend to produce wilder results, but they can also be successfully saved. Some hybrid varieties are seedless or infertile, but that is not the norm. Dehybridising hybrids is an exciting practice in which over several years of careful selection, you can breed the plant's best properties into stable seed lines. To learn more, we highly recommend Carol Deppe's excellent book, *Breed Your Own Vegetable Varieties*.

Growing considerations

Growing to preserve the seed variety

If you want to save seeds to preserve the seed line, there are a few more rules to follow, compared with saving the seeds for personal use.

Grow a minimum number of plants

To properly preserve a seed line, you will need to grow a minimum number of plants to maintain good genetic diversity within the seed line. This minimum number changes between different types and helps ensure that the plants stay vigorous. If you only save seeds from a small number of plants, it is likely your seed line will deteriorate over time. The minimum number of plants to save seed ranges from 12 to 200 depending on the vegetable, as we detail in the table on page 291.

Growing a larger number of plants than you need to ensure good plant vigour allows you to remove plants that show unwanted

Left Yellow chard going to seed.

characteristics, in a process called roguing. When you save seeds, it is an opportunity to continuously select the best plants to breed from. Plants should be closely observed throughout the season, and plants with unwanted characteristics should be removed before they flower, so their genetics won't be transferred. Plants that quickly bolt and go to seed are best not kept for seed. Saving seed from these plants will increase the tendency of the next generation to bolt.

By choosing the most vigorous, tastiest, healthiest plants, these characteristics will ensure your next generation of plants will be as good, if not better than the one before.

Avoid eating your best plants

Avoid eating your very best plants, as they are the best plants to save seeds from. With tomatoes and some other fruits, you can eat the fruit and save the seeds at the same time. With pumpkins, the seeds will continue to ripen for two to three months after harvest, so if the variety stores well and you have the patience, waiting will result in higher-quality seeds. Many other vegetables require you to let the plants grow past their edible stage in order to save their seeds.

You can harvest a few leaves without affecting the health of your plants, but it is best to leave the plants you are saving seeds from alone to let them grow strong in peace. Ideally, you should eat small- to medium-sized plants that have characteristics that you don't like, and leave the bigger ones alone. It's hard to do, but it will mean the next generation of seeds will come from the healthiest, strongest plants.

Avoid cross-pollination

Avoid cross-pollination between seed varieties of the same vegetable. If plants from different varieties of the same species are grown in proximity to each other, the pollen can cross, and hybrids will be created. Although all plant varieties can cross within their species, self-pollinated plants (also referred to as inbreeding plants) tend to cross less, as pollination generally occurs before the flowers open. You can save seeds from self-pollinating varieties grown next to each other, such as tomatoes, beans, peas and lettuce. If possible, it is safer to have a 6 metre (20 feet) distance between varieties, as some pollination can still occur, such as when bees eat or tear open a flower's petals and deposit pollen from another plant.

Plants that are pollinated by wind (such as beets, corn and spinach) and insects (most vegetables), especially by bees, need to have another plant's pollen to develop seeds and are referred to as outbreeding plants. To save seeds from outbreeding varieties, you will benefit from at least a 1.6 km (1 mile) distance between varieties, which can be decreased if the landscape and vegetation make it harder for insects and wind to travel.

There are methods you can use to grow more than one variety and save the seeds from both. Hand pollination is possible for Cucurbits, especially large, flowering species such as pumpkins or courgettes, but it's not a common practice in the home garden. An easier way to save seeds from plants that can cross is to use time to your advantage, and sow them six to eight weeks apart, so their flowering seasons won't overlap. In this situation, you would be safe to save the seeds from the first fruits of the first variety, and the late fruits of the second variety.

Be aware that some vegetables look different and have different names, but are actually the same species, and will still cross. For example, broccoli, cabbage and cauliflower will cross with one another, and chard and beets will cross with each other too. The opposite can also be true, and vegetables that look similar or have a similar name are actually different species and will not cross. These include the three types of squash (pepo, maxima and moschata); you can grow one of each variety without the risk of cross-pollination.

Lastly, some vegetables are close enough to their wild ancestors from which they were cultivated that they would likely cross with each other. The most relevant example is the wild carrot, which will readily cross with the domestic carrot if it is close by.

The Abundant Garden

Seed-saving information for common vegetables

Vegetable	Pollination	Self-pollinating (S) / Outbreeding (O)	Minimum isolation distance between varieties	Minimum plant numbers for genetic maintenance
Basil	insects	O	1.6 km (1 mile)	80
Bean	self and insects	S	3 m (10 feet)	20
Beet	wind	O	3.2 km (2 miles)	80
Broad beans	self and insects	S and O	800 m (0.5 miles)	40
Broccoli, cabbage and cauliflower	insects	O	1.6 km (1 mile)	80
Capsicum and chilli peppers	self and insects	S and O	50 m (160 feet) capsicum, 800 m (0.5 mile) chilli	20 capsicum, 40 chilli
Carrots	insects	O	1.6 km (1 mile)	200
Celery	insects	O	1.6 km (1 mile)	80
Coriander	insects	O	1.6 km (1 mile)	80
Corn	wind	O	1.6 km (1 mile)	200
Courgette, cucumber	insects	O	1.6 km (1 mile)	12
Eggplant	insects	O	1.6 km (1 mile)	80
Endive	self	S	3 m (10 feet)	12
Fennel	insects	O	1.6 km (1 mile)	80
Kale, kohlrabi	insects	O	1.6 km (1 mile)	80
Leek, onion	insects	O	1.6 km (1 mile)	80 leek, 200 onion
Lettuce	self	S	3 m (10 feet)	12
Parsley	insects	O	1.6 km (1 mile)	80
Parsnip	insects	O	1.6 km (1 mile)	80
Pea	self	S	3 m (10 feet)	12
Pumpkin, rock melon, squash, watermelon	insects	O	1.6 km (1 mile)	12
Radish, rocket, turnip	insects	O	1.6 km (1 mile)	80
Spinach	wind	O	3.2 km (2 miles)	80
Tomato	self and insects	S	6 m (20 feet)	12

Left Bean emerging from the soil.

Space

When growing plants to save their seed, plants that go to seed will need to be allowed to develop to their full size, but can generally be grown with the same spacing that you would regularly use. Many plants will need vertical space for their large stalks and seed heads. If your plants are closely spaced, harvest the ones you don't want to save seeds from, freeing more space for the full-sized stage of the remaining plants. Once the plants reach their full size, you will likely need to add stakes and strings for extra support for tall plants. Plants from the following families will likely need staking: carrot family (Apiaceae), cabbage family (Brassicaceae), lettuce family (Asteraceae), beet family (Amaranthaceae) and onion family (Alliaceae).

Timing and watering

Spring and early summer are generally the best times to grow plants for seed saving, as this will give the plants enough time to grow and set seeds during the dry summer. Plants need similar amounts of water to be able to develop seeds as they need throughout the rest of their growing cycle. Once the plants are in the last couple of weeks of their growing cycle, it is best to avoid overhead watering, to avoid spoiling the seeds or causing them to germinate.

Non-fruiting plants that go seed will usually need to stay six to eight weeks longer in the bed, to allow them to reach full maturity. Some fruits such as capsicum, squash, melons and tomatoes will be ripe when the fruit itself is ready to eat. Other fruits, such as eggplants, cucumber and courgette, will need to be left on the plants to over-ripen beyond their edible stage, for their seeds to fully mature and be ready for harvest.

While most plants can be grown as annuals and will set seeds within the same season, some plants do need to be exposed to cold weather or experience another growing season before setting seeds. This includes carrots, beets and cabbages, which all need to experience at least eight weeks of temperatures below 10°C (50°F) to induce going to seed. To achieve this you can grow them in

Below Snowball cauliflower (white), violet Sicilian (purple) and romanesco (green).

autumn so the plants can overwinter, or plant them in early spring under cloches. Onions are biennial plants that will always need to be planted as bulbs so they will set seeds.

Harvesting and processing seeds

There are two main methods to process seeds, depending on the type of plant.

Dry seeds

The seeds of most plants develop on stalks. It can sometimes be a bit tricky to decide when to harvest the seeds. Once the seeds are close to maturity, close observation will help you find the sweet spot, where the seeds are ripe and ready to be harvested, but before they disconnect and fall to the ground. Often you will find yourself harvesting the seeds over a few weeks, as not all the plant's seeds will be ready at the same time. If rain or a frost is expected and the seeds are almost ripe, it is best to harvest them before the rain or frost so that they don't spoil.

If you are harvesting the plants when the seeds are ripe, you can cut the plants relatively close to the seed heads or only collect the pods. We come out to the garden with large paper bags and old pillowcases, and collect the seed heads directly into them. The same bag or pillowcase can be used over the few weeks you harvest the same seeds. Write the name of the plant variety on the paper bag or slip a piece of paper into the pillowcase, so you know what seeds you have collected later on.

After harvesting, the seeds will need to dry out. Storing them in paper or fabric and leaving them in a well-ventilated area will help moisture to escape while keeping the seeds contained. It's best to dry your plants quickly so they don't get mouldy. To assist with quick drying, you can expose the seeds to direct sun for a few days, especially if they are still a bit green or moist.

If you are harvesting the plants a little early because rain is forecast, it is better to harvest whole plants instead of just the seed heads. This way, the goodness from the plant body can move into the seeds, increasing their quality. If we are doing this with large quantities of plants, we use a large sheet rather than a pillowcase. Once the sun is shining, bring the plants out to dry, but remember to put them back undercover in the late afternoon or cover them with a tarp so that the night moisture doesn't dampen the seeds.

Seeds will often take a week or so to completely dry to the point that they are ready for long-term storage. When pressed, the dry seeds should break or snap, rather than bend or mush. Once the seeds are dry, they can be separated from the stalks and sieved from the plant material, in a process called threshing. You can use your hands (wear gloves!), though our preferred method is to step on them with a little dance.

To separate the seeds from the debris and chaff, in a process called winnowing, you can use a kitchen or garden sieve. Since the seeds are usually heavier than the small pieces of chaff, place the seeds in a bowl and blow on the seeds and chaff mix to clean the seeds. For large amounts of seeds, you can use a fan on a low setting to blow the chaff away, though we suggest placing a sheet or tarp on the ground first. With seeds like lettuce, which are a bit harder to completely clean, we just save them with a bit of chaff, since they can still be sown that way.

Wet seeds

Saving seeds from fruits is relatively straightforward. Once the fruit is ripe or mature enough for seed collection, it can be cut, and the seeds scooped or squeezed out. Once separated from the flesh, you are left with a choice: whether or not to ferment the seeds.

If you are using the seeds in the following season, you will generally be safe enough to scoop the seeds, wash them to remove as much pulp as possible and then dry them. To make the pulp separation easier, you can soak the seeds and pulp for up to eight hours before washing it. Let the seeds dry a little in a sieve, and then you can either leave them there, or place them on a tray or on any non-stick surface. After most of the water has drained from the sieve, you can also put the seeds on a paper towel, but they may stick to it. If you are drying them on a sieve or a tray, stir them frequently to prevent them from sticking to the surface and to encourage even drying. To dry the seeds quickly, place them in a well-ventilated area. You could also place the seeds in the sun but be careful they don't get too hot, or they will cook.

If you want to save the seeds for longer than next season, improve their germination rate and get rid of seed-borne diseases, fermenting the seeds and their coating will be a better option. We suggest starting with fermenting tomato and cucumber seeds, which benefit the most from this process.

To ferment the seeds, mimic what would have naturally happened to the fruits in nature.

The seeds and pulp can be left in a jar for two to three days to ferment, mixed with a little of water (but not much as it can delay the fermentation process). Stir the seeds twice a day, until a white mould develops on the surface or the seed cases separate from the seeds. If you leave the seeds to ferment for too long, they could germinate or even rot.

Once the fermentation is complete, add water and mix vigorously. The viable seeds tend to sink to the bottom, and any floating material and non-viable seeds can be skimmed off. Wash the viable seeds thoroughly and let them dry as set out above.

Labelling and Storage

Once your seeds are dry and dormant, extend their shelf life by storing them in conditions that reduce their respiration rate and maintain their vigour. An airtight container in a cool, dry and dark cupboard will work well. Moisture is the leading cause of spoiled seeds, so storing your seeds when they are thoroughly dry is the best way to extend their storage life. Glass jars with good rubber seals are the best containers to use, as plastic bags are not sufficiently air tight. You can place many seeds in different Ziploc bags inside the same jar, and add silica gel sachets or even rice to absorb any moisture still present.

Labelling your seeds is essential; the opposite to forgetting is writing down! On the container, write the date, variety, seed source, and any other details you feel might be valuable, such as seed quality, any potential cross-pollination, number of plants and so on.

The quality of your seed storage will directly affect the health of the seeds and the vigour the plants will display when you grow them in the garden. When stored properly, many vegetable seeds can last for two to four years, with a reasonable germination rate. Germination rate and seed vigour decrease over time, and although some seeds will continue to germinate when the germination rate is low, the seed vigour will be low as well. It is best to grow plants from fresh seeds only, as low-vigour seeds produce weaker plants. Aim for at least a 70 per cent germination rate for the best results.

Freezing seeds can also significantly extend their shelf life. Some seeds will even germinate better after being frozen. Additionally, insects and some seed-borne diseases will die once the seeds have been stored for a few days in the freezer. It is essential to make sure seeds are thoroughly dry before freezing, or the moisture will cause the cells to burst. Before using the seeds, let them thaw at room temperature for at least a day, as otherwise moisture will condense on the seeds and decrease their storage life.

Shelf life of vegetable seeds

Seed	Expected storage life in years
Basil	3–4
Bean	3–5
Beet	2–5
Broccoli, cabbage, cauliflower	3–5
Capsicum, peppers	2–5
Carrots	2–3
Celery	3–5
Coriander	2–4
Corn	2–5
Courgette, cucumber	4–6
Eggplant	4–5
Endive	4–5
Fennel	2–3
Kale, kohlrabi	3–5
Leek, onion	2–3
Lettuce	2–5
Parsley	1–3
Parsnip	1
Pea	2–4
Pumpkin, rock melon, squash, watermelon	4–6
Radish, rocket, turnip	4–6
Spinach	2–4
Tomato	4–6

Chapter 14.
Fermenting and preserving produce

Fermenting is an exciting way to preserve the abundance of your garden. It is easy to do and adds a great variety of flavours and textures to every meal.

Fermenting vegetables

Fermentation also enhances your produce's nutritional qualities.

The easiest and most accessible type of fermentation is lacto-fermentation. It can be done in any kitchen, at room temperature, with nothing more than water, salt and a clean jar. Lacto-fermentation is a process that involves lactic acid bacteria, most commonly Lactobacillus. These bacteria metabolise the sugars in the food and create lactic acid. In turn, the acidic environment preserves the food, preventing potentially harmful microorganisms and mould. Lactobacillus bacteria are literally everywhere, so there is no need to buy them at a shop.

Eating fermented foods is healthy because the probiotic properties of the live bacteria in the food are beneficial to our digestive system. The more diverse the range of foods we ferment, the broader the spectrum of bacteria that will come and feast on them. The natural, complex bacterial community that naturally occurs when making sauerkraut, for example, is far superior to any probiotic in a capsule. That's why fermented food is consumed on a daily basis in traditional cultures all around the world.

Part of the beauty of fermenting foods is that you can use almost anything to make ferments. It doesn't need to be the prettiest carrot to make the cut, however it is still best to use fresh vegetables at their prime. You can make a single plant ferment or combine several plants and herbs together, used whole or cut to any shape or size for interesting flavours, colours and textures. Making lacto-fermented foods is a graceful process, as your kitchen shelves start filling up with jars of vividly coloured vegetables, happily fermenting in salt water.

To ensure the salt-tolerant Lactobacillus species will be the dominant bacteria in your ferments, add around 3 per cent salt to your vegetable brine. This percentage is somewhat flexible, and you can add or reduce the salt content to suit your taste, or with the season. We measure our brine in cups. In the summer, when the warm environment encourages quicker fermentation, we usually stick to 1 teaspoon of salt per 1 cup water. In the winter, when fermentation is slower, and there is more chance for the ferment to be contaminated, we use more salt, usually about 1.5–2 teaspoons per 1 cup water. Use natural sea salt without preservatives and anti-clotting agents, as they might prevent the lacto bacteria from flourishing.

It's important to keep the vegetables submerged in the brine, as this creates an anaerobic environment. If any part of the vegetable pops out of the brine and is exposed to the air, the vegetable piece can be colonised by mould or competing bacteria and can contaminate the whole jar. To submerge the vegetables, you will need to keep them weighed down. You can sterilise a smooth river stone to place on top of them, buy a special fermentation weight, use a piece of ceramic or a small plate. As long as you can manage to keep both the veggies and whatever you are using to weigh them down under the brine, you're fine.

Leave a gap of a few centimetres of air between the top of the liquid and the lid of your jar. This prevents an overflow of liquid that bubbles up during the fermentation process from spilling out of the jar. If a lot of brine has spilled out, you should replenish it to ensure the vegetables remain fully covered. In any case, place a plate or bowl under the jars to keep the area clean.

When judging whether the ferment is still good to eat, use your senses. If it smells rotten or if there is green mould, don't eat it, as the entire jar will be affected. If you are not sure how ferments should taste, purchase a live (non-pasteurised) raw ferment at your local organic shop.

When you first introduce fermented foods to your diet, do it gradually and in small amounts. These are potent foods that will help you develop a healthier gut microbiome, but it can be uncomfortable if you overwhelm your body with them all in one go.

Before you start

To prepare ferments, all you need is a bit of counter space, a chopping board, a sharp knife, glass jars with lids and weights to submerge the vegetables. To keep the ferments submerged, we like to use a clean, smooth river stone that fits neatly in the jar, but there are many other options that you can make, repurpose or buy specifically for this purpose. Make sure the jar lids are in good condition, as exposed metal can react with the brine as it acidifies. You can buy simple silicon airlock lids that fit a standard preserving jar ring, plastic lids, or just cover the container with cheesecloth to keep insects away.

We always follow a few safety measures to make sure our ferments are safe to eat. Hot water and soap are our friends; there is no need to use sanitisers. We make sure the surface and equipment we use to prepare ferments (such as a knife, chopping board, jars and weights) are thoroughly clean. You can use a hot dishwasher cycle to clean the jars, utensils and weights, as long as you are planning to use them as soon as the dishwasher has finished its cycle. We also clean our hands, including under the fingernails, and make sure the vegetables we are using are completely clean from soil particles.

When you open a jar of fermented vegetables, it is important to use clean serving utensils, and to absolutely avoid double-dipping. We find that after we start consuming a ferment, it is best to keep it in the fridge, ensuring the brine still covers the vegetables.

Right Fermenting vegetables in brine.

Fermenting and preserving produce

Recipes

Vegetables in brine

This recipe works with practically any and every vegetable, but generally firm vegetables produce a better-textured ferment. We prefer using young vegetables such as cucumbers and green cherry tomatoes or vegetables that are naturally firm regardless of harvest stage such as carrots, radishes and kohlrabi.

For lacto-fermented sauces, spreads or condiments you could use softer vegetables using this same recipe.

1. Wash vegetables to remove any soil particles and prepare them according to your preference. Small root vegetables, such as salad turnips and radishes, can be fermented whole. Larger vegetables such as carrots, butternuts and kohlrabi can be sliced, diced or cut into sticks, which are often popular with kids. You can use one type of vegetable or a mixture.
2. Place vegetables in a clean jar. Laying the jar on its side makes it easier to stack sticks neatly. To add flavours and colours, use your favourite herbs, spices and even flower petals, such as rosemary, garlic, ginger, lemon, coriander, cardamom seeds, juniper berries or calendula petals. Try new combinations or stick to traditional pairings; it's up to you.
3. Make the brine. For 1 cup water, add 1–2 teaspoons of salt. More salt will result in slower fermentation and crunchier veggies.
4. Submerge the vegetables completely in the brine and weigh them down. Remember that any vegetable exposed to air becomes a breeding ground for mould and other bacteria that will spoil the ferment. The top of the jar should have an air gap to control the overflow. Cover with a lid or cheesecloth to stop insects from contaminating the ferment.
5. Place out of direct light in a cool location, with a plate underneath in case any liquids spill over.
6. Check your ferment regularly. If the brine is low, top it up. If you see floating bits, fish them out or push them back down with a freshly cleaned spoon.

After two to three weeks, the ferment will be ready to eat. You can leave it to ferment for longer, which will make the taste sourer and the texture softer over time. When the ferment reaches the right sourness and texture to your liking, put it in the fridge so the fermentation slows down. Ferments in the fridge, kept submerged in their brine, will keep for months.

Variations and suggestions

- To make traditional dill pickles, ferment whole young cucumbers with bay leaf, dill, garlic and chilli. Soak the cucumbers in icy water for an hour before adding them to the jar to make them hard and crunchy. This same seasoning combination is also great for fermenting watermelon rinds!
- To colour any ferment pink, simply add a piece of beetroot to the mix.
- To add crunch to your ferments, add tannin-rich leaves such as grape leaf or oak leaf to the mix.

Sauerkraut

Sauerkraut is one of our favourite ferments. It is a popular food in one form or another in many parts of the world. We love making it and eating it so much that we sometimes refer to our cabbage beds as our 'sauerkraut patch'.

Sauerkraut is basically another variation of vegetables in brine, but instead of making the brine from water, you use salt and your hands to draw the brine liquids from the cabbage itself.

1. Slice the cabbages and place in a bowl.
2. Sprinkle 1 tablespoon salt per medium-size cabbage.
3. Knead the cabbage in a bowl with the heel of your hands, making a satisfying crunching sound. Keep going until the cabbage is soft and liquids accumulate in the bottom of the bowl, which can take 5–10 minutes per cabbage.
4. Pack the cabbage tightly into a container, using your knuckles or a wooden spoon to push the cabbages firmly down until there are no air gaps and the brine covers the

cabbage. If you are short of liquid, add a brine made of 1 teaspoon salt per 1 cup water.

5. Weigh the cabbage down to keep it submerged. Cover with a cloth or a lid with an airlock. Place the container on a plate or a tray.

6. During the bubbly fermentation stage, sauerkraut can lose significant amounts of brine. Keep an eye on the levels of liquid so you can top it up with more brine when needed.

7. The sauerkraut will be ready to eat within three weeks.

You can also layer chopped fruit or vegetables, such as apples or radishes, between the layers of cabbage, and add spices to your liking. Our favourite variations are:

- Mixing green and red cabbage for pink-coloured sauerkraut.
- Adding 1 teaspoon caraway seeds per cabbage.
- Adding calendula petals mixed in with the cabbage as it is packed into the jar.
- Adding a thumb of sliced ginger per cabbage.

Beet kvass

Beet kvass is a liquid version of vegetables in brine. It's outrageous how simple it is!

1. Cut a small- to medium-sized beetroot into quarters, skin and all. Place in a 1-litre jar.

2. Make enough brine to fill up the jar by mixing 1–2 teaspoons salt per 1 litre water.

3. The beet kvass will be ready in one to two weeks.

4. The deep red liquid is full of probiotic bacteria, and can be drunk as is, or better yet, mixed into smoothies. We tend to add it to berry smoothies, where it adds a vibrant colour.

Above Beetroot.

Right Sauerkraut with radish, beets, dill flowers and calendula petals.

Kraut, calendula radish, red/gold beets, dill flowers. 8/1

Pickling and preserving

In addition to fermenting, you can also stock up the pantry with delicious vegetable preserves and pickles. We love preserving the taste of summer vegetables so that we can enjoy them over winter. We often purposefully grow crops in order to preserve them, and when we have surplus vegetables and a bit of time, into the pot they go.

Pickling vegetables

We like to pickle vegetables using a similar method to fermenting vegetables in brine. The main difference is that we add vinegar to the salt brine. We prefer not to boil the brine or to add sugar. Pickling vegetables adds a unique taste and a crunchy texture.

1. Cut vegetables and mix in a bowl, with spices to taste.
2. Place vegetable mix in a jar.
3. Make a brine by adding 1.5 teaspoons salt and 0.25 cup vinegar per 1 cup water. Pour over the vegetable mix. You can use any vinegar you want; organic apple cider vinegar is a good choice.
4. Add a stone to submerge the mix and place lid.
5. The pickled vegetables will be ready to eat after a few days, but for the best flavour, leave them at room temperature for a week or two. Pickled vegetables will keep in the fridge for up to two months.

Our favourite variation of pickled vegetables is made with:

- 1 small cabbage, cut into small bite-size strips
- 1 cauliflower, cut into bite-size florets
- 1 broccoli, cut into bite-size florets
- 4 carrots, sliced at a sharp angle into elongated ovals
- 2 courgettes, sliced at a sharp angle into elongated ovals
- 2 capsicums, cut into squares
- 3 small onions, sliced
- 4 garlic cloves, sliced
- 5 cm (2 inch) of thumb-width ginger
- 2 chillies

Below Strawberry patch.

- 1 tablespoon mustard seeds
- 1 teaspoon ground turmeric
- a few allspice seeds

Strawberry sauce

A household favourite, strawberry sauce is one of many fruit preserves we make every year. Unlike most traditional fruit preserves, this low-sugar recipe does not set. We have found that adding a small amount of honey creates a delicious and versatile sauce. We like using it not only with desserts but also as a healthy alternative to tomato sauce (ketchup) when eating sausages and other savoury dishes.

1. Cut the tops off the strawberries and place in a pot. Add a bit of water to cover the bottom of the pot, about 1–2 cm (0.4–0.8 inches) deep.
2. Bring to a slow boil, then keep simmering on a low heat without a lid, frequently stirring, until it reaches your desired texture. You can take the pot off the heat after 20 minutes simmering, or leave it for hours to reduce. You can also cook it in a slow cooker or solar cooker.
3. Remove from the heat. Add 1 teaspoon honey or sugar per cup of sauce.
4. While hot, pour into glass jars that have been sterilised and kept warm and place the lid.
5. Place jars in a pot, cover with water, bring the pot to a boil, and keep on low heat for 10 minutes.
6. Cool the filled jars. The jars will store well at room temperature, with no refrigeration, for several years, though we're sure you'll eat it within a few months. Our largest batch of strawberry sauce was 40 litres, and it didn't make it to the following summer!

The Abundant Garden

Shakshuka base (summer vegetables preserve)

Shakshuka is one of our favourite preserves to have available for winter. This recipe comes from Yotam's grandma, Blanche, who always serves shakshuka as a first course at the family's Friday night meals, as a dip with fresh pita bread.

Shakshuka is perfect for making when the garden is overflowing with capsicum, eggplants and tomatoes. You can use it later as an upgraded version of tomato paste, or as the base to make shakshuka with eggs.

Ingredients for a 6-litre pot:

- 6–7 large onions, diced
- 4 large capsicum, diced
- 3–6 chillies, depending on taste
- 3 large or 4 medium to large eggplants, cut into small pieces
- 10 large tomatoes, or equivalent of any variety, diced
- salt
- 4 tablespoons sweet paprika

1. In a large pot, sauté onions in oil of your choice until they turn yellow.
2. Add the capsicum, chilli, eggplant and tomatoes, and bring to a slow boil without any additional water.
3. Add the salt and sweet paprika and cook on low heat for about an hour.
4. Remove from the stove.
5. While hot, pour into glass jars that have been sterilised and preheated and place the lid. We sanitise the jars by slowly bringing them to a boil in a large pot of water, and keeping them warm to avoid rapid temperature changes when filling them with sauce that can break the glass jars.
6. To pasteurise and can the shakshuka, fit the full jars inside in a large pot. Cover the jars with water, slowly bringing the pot to a boil, and simmering on low heat for 10 minutes. The jars will store well at room temperature, with no refrigeration, for a couple of years.

Left Preparing and enjoying shakshuka.

7. Yotam's grandma cooks about 20 litres of shakshuka at a time, lets it cool, then fills enough bags to freeze for a six-month supply. She fills the bags three-quarters full, and places them in the freezer with a bit of space between them so they don't freeze together.

To make shakshuka with eggs, a simply delicious Middle Eastern dish, use the following recipe:

1. In a deep pan or wide pot, cook the shakshuka base and bring it to the boil. Preserved shakshuka might be slightly too thick, in which case you will need to add a bit of water.
2. Add olive oil, spices and herbs for flavour. We love including plenty of basil and parsley.
3. Once the shakshuka boils, break eggs into a cup one at a time, 2 eggs per person. Use a spoon to make room for the eggs in the sauce. Carefully place each egg in the pan, so that it is nicely embedded in the shakshuka base.
4. Place a lid on the pan and let the eggs poach for a few minutes on low heat. We prefer to enjoy shakshuka while the eggs yolks are a bit runny.
5. Serve immediately. This dish is often enjoyed with a fresh loaf of bread or pita bread, which you can use to mop up the sauce.

Acknowledgements

We first want to acknowledge the people of Hauraki whose traditions of growing food and caring for the land have always been here.

We are very privileged to have been so warmly welcomed to Pakaraka Farm by Harry Parke and Jeanette Fitzsimons. Their wisdom and friendship are invaluable. Harry, it is a pleasure to live, talk and teach gardening with you. Jeanette, we miss you.

We are grateful for the work of the fabulous team at Allen & Unwin: Jenny Hellen, the publishing director, who saw the potential of a great gardening book and has worked with us from inception throughout to make this book what it is; Leonie Freeman, the project editor who took great care of all the many details that needed to be brought together and in time!; the awesome editor Tracey Wogan; and skilful designer Megan van Staden.

Thank you to photographer Jane Ussher, who took beautiful portraits of our family, and gorgeous images of the garden. And to our multi-talented illustrator and garden-hand Bianca Rocca who managed to produce such beautiful artwork while taking in the many technical details we asked her to adhere to.

Thank you to our beloved family who are always supportive of us. Special thanks to our daughters, Lily and Dina, for being patient with us during the writing of this book and for being their awesome selves. To aunty Keren who tested out the shakshuka recipe in her kitchen in New York for her help in refining this recipe.

Thank you to our friends, colleagues and community for providing such a rich local gardening culture, and for sharing your enthusiasm and discoveries, and sometimes also seeds and plant material.

To everyone who has come to visit, learn and stay with us at Pakaraka Farm, thank you for taking part in our journey.

Last but not least, a huge thank you to you, the reader. We hope that you have found the information in this book helpful. May your garden thrive.

Niva & Yotam Kay.

Index

Page numbers in **bold** refer to the main entries for each vegetable.

The Abundant Garden